FISHING
REFLECTIONS

Thoughts on salmon, trout and grayling fishing

FISHING REFLECTIONS

Thoughts on salmon, trout and grayling fishing

Reg Righyni

Edited by John Winter

SWAN·HILL
PRESS

First published in the UK in 1995
by Swan Hill Press an imprint of Airlife Publishing Ltd

British Library Cataloguing in Publication Data
  A catalogue record for this book
  is available from the British Library

ISBN 1 85310 444 2

Typeset by Hewer Text Composition Services, Edinburgh
Printed by Livesey Ltd, Shrewsbury

Swan Hill Press
an imprint of Airlife Publishing Ltd
101 Longden Road, Shrewsbury SY3 9EB

FOR BETTY

Dedicated to the memory of a
very dear friend and mentor
for the many happy hours
spent together.

Contents

Contents

R.V.Righyni

R.V. Righyni, universally known as Reg, was one of the best practical anglers of his era. Born at Bradford on 27 June 1912, his father, an officer in the French army, died from wounds sustained during the 1914–18 war, and he was brought up by his mother, a Yorkshire girl, and her parents.

A very positive man of great energy, intelligence and stamina, he entered the wool trade, quickly making his mark on the Bradford Wool Exchange and becoming an internationally respected wool broker.

In the Second World War, as a commissioned officer in the Royal Artillery, he took part in the D-Day landings and the liberation of Europe, an interlude of great personal significance in view of his family background.

My first meeting with Reg occurred back in the late 'fifties. Already he had established a reputation as a highly competent all-round angler and was considered to be a sound exponent on salmon, sea-trout, trout and grayling fishing. His apprenticeship to coarse fishing had started way back in his early years when he was taken under the wing of the late J.H.R.Bazley. 'Baz' enjoyed great fame as a match fisherman in those days and some of Reg's early water lore was learned at the feet of this master and he always acknowledged his indebtedness to 'Baz'.

It was shortly after our meeting that Reg invited me to join him for a day on his beat on the Lune. Frankly, I cannot recall if I caught anything on my first outing with him, but I know that I was sufficiently impressed by the potential to wish to be asked again. In 1965 I and a friend were asked to take a rod on the beat and thus it was over the years that we became good friends.

Fly-fishing was his main interest. He had few equals at trout and grayling fishing in the North of England waters, of which the Wharfe was specially dear to him. He caught his first salmon in 1929, from the Thurso, on a visit with a party of the Bradford Waltonians. For many years he concentrated on salmon, having the good fortune to fish the best beats when there were plenty of fish. By 1965 Reg had crystallized many of his thoughts on salmon fishing and gave us his first book *Salmon Taking Times*. In it, Reg expressed some firm opinions on why and when a salmon might take your lure. He was a great man for theories – particularly when related to salmon fishing. I feel that *Salmon Taking Times* made an important contribution to our knowledge of how we might try to catch them.

If Reg had another angling obsession it was his great love of grayling fishing. Indeed, by 1968 his book *Grayling* was published. It was a small but important work, which was to demonstrate that of all our game fish species the grayling alone is the only one which has not suffered (or benefited from for that matter) any genetic interference.

His retirement was really a second career – as angling consultant, author, speaker and tackle designer. He designed some excellent and justly popular game fishing rods in an exciting era of changing materials and construction methods. In grayling circles he will be remembered for the *Righyni grayling-float*.

In his latter years Reg confined his angling activity almost exclusively to the grayling. Through his love of grayling fishing he was the moving spirit behind the formation of the Grayling Society. He frequently wrote to tell me, with some pride, that he had added yet another grayling river to those on which he had already caught grayling. I recall that he notched up 150 such rivers and there cannot be many grayling fishermen who can claim that.

A swift, safe and law-abiding driver of Bristol cars, he travelled widely in response to requests to speak to angling clubs. He always encouraged the highest standards of sportsmanship and respect for the fish. Modern and forward looking in his approach to technological advances, he cared passionately that the best traditions of the sport should be passed on to the next generation. Above all, he was always a true and devoted friend and my lasting thoughts of him are that he was just about the kindest man I ever met.

Arthur Oglesby

Editor's Introduction

On 5 July 1987, the angling world suffered the sudden loss of one of its most knowledgable members with the passing of R.V. Righyni, Reg, to the many anglers who came to know him through his 'fishing talks' and attendances at many angling fairs throughout the country over the years.

I was one of those who were privileged to become a close friend of Reg's, and although it was but for a relatively short time, in those eight short years I gained knowledge which would have taken me many, many years to do so on my own. Many were the days and nights spent in his cottage at Barbon discussing every aspect of angling, from conservation to tactics and river improvement to his 'oxygen theory'. Over this period it was as though the veil of mystery which clouds many anglers view on salmon fishing, indeed all angling for game fish, was slowly but surely removed.

Following Reg's passing, Betty, his widow, gave me some old copies of the fishing magazine *Creel*, a magazine which was popular in the 1960s. When I read through these I realised that here, in print, were many of the topics discussed on those happy days at 'Oakleigh'. It became apparent that many of today's anglers would not have had the benefit of reading these very interesting, educating articles and those published in other, earlier angling periodicals, and that this would be another sad loss to the angling world. I thought that it would benefit all of today's anglers, and no doubt future generations of anglers too, if these articles were published in book form and dedicated to the memory of a man whose knowledge, love and dedication to angling has placed him amongst other great anglers such as Skues and Halford.

I am eternally thankful to Betty for the wonderful warm hospitality shown to me on my many stays at 'Oakleigh', for her endless patience and understanding when Reg and I were in full flight, so to speak, on angling topics. This kindness made me feel 'at home' at Barbon and the happy memories of those days will remain with me for the remainder of my life.

I am greatly indebted to many people for assisting me in compiling this collection and special thanks are given to Dermott Wilson, Arthur Oglesby Mike Pritchard and Barry Lloyd for the many photographs they supplied. I also thank William Collins Ltd, Bruce & Walker Ltd, *Trout and Salmon* magazine, The Grayling Society and many others for providing material to enable this work to be completed.

All I wish is that the reader will be able to remove the veil on many of the problems we all as anglers face from time to time. If this collection allows each reader to solve one problem or mystery, then I feel that the wisdom of Reg will have been passed on to present and future generations and that I have made a small repayment to the priceless wealth of knowledge gained from a friendship which was sadly too short.

Finally, I would like to thank Peter Patrick, Barry Lloyd, John Castle, Alex Pickover and Frank Preston for allowing me to take over the rod which Reg had fished at Newton Hall on his beloved Lune for thirty-five years.

John Winter

Part One

Salmon

Chapter 1

Hooking Salmon with the Fly

One famous author who writes with commanding assurance tells the salmon fly-fisher that he should never, never, strike or tighten on a fish. His words make it sound very simple to give an abundance of line so that the downstream belly draws the iron into the corner of the salmon's mouth without any movement of the rod. This advice is presented with such insistence that one is led to believe that it is sheer inefficiency – and very lucky, too – ever to land a salmon that is hooked anywhere other than the angle of the jaws.

Another writer who enjoys great popularity, and is acknowledged to be a highly successful and versatile salmon fisher, is equally convinced that the most effective method is to strike as soon as the draw on the line is sufficient to establish that the fish has closed his mouth on the fly.

These conflicting ideas are each supported by the strongest of arguments. The novice must find it very difficult to decide which of the two experts he should attempt to emulate. And it must be still more confusing for him when he finds that the majority of the rank and file of salmon fishers pay no apparent heed to either of these exhortations. The method which is practised almost universally is to give the fish a couple of yards of slack line in any or all circumstances and then tighten on him. This is not – as it might appear at first glance – a compromise between the other two methods. In principle it is a denial of both.

However, no one would claim this popular system to be perfect. Offers are missed and fish are often poorly hooked and lost. But references to the high risk of such misfortunes at times – particularly from early summer onwards – usually produce the answer that, over all, this method has been found to be more reliable than either of the opposing ones advocated by the experts.

15

Is there then, a way of hooking and landing a better proportion of the salmon that take a fly? In search of the answer to this I have done a great deal of experimenting over a period of a few years. I have engaged in trials at all times of the season, and on a variety of rivers, of all the methods of which I have read or heard. This has resulted in spells of missing offer after offer and losing many fish, but now it enables me to comment on the problem without having to resort to second-hand information.

The first and most vital question requiring to be answered is whether it is true that, having taken a fly, the salmon always grips it firmly until he gets back to his lie – providing, of course, that sufficient slack line has been given – and that he cannot get rid of the iron without the strain of the water on the line drawing it through the angle of the jaws, where it is nearly certain to get a secure hold?

In the case of fresh run fish in spring, it would be difficult to refute this. But it is often beyond the powers of even very skilful anglers to give sufficient line quickly enough to ensure that the fish does not feel resistance. And there is no doubt that salmon will either spit the fly out, or release their hold and let it be drawn clear, if they feel too much pull from the line. But I am certain that grilse in particular, small summer salmon, and to some extent most stale fish, do not hang onto the fly with anywhere near the same determination as the fresh run springer. They are much more subject to spitting the fly out before sufficient downstream belly has been able to form to ensure the hooking of the fish.

The second principal problem is whether it is possible in any circumstances to ensure that the fish will be hooked in that desirable position in the corner of the mouth, as it is supposed to be achieved by giving line and avoiding tightening. The answer, unfortunately, is no! Especially with the small, extremely sharp hooks used when fishing greased line, the point often penetrates and gets fixed before the iron can reach the corner of the mouth. Frequently when I have given many yards of line and waited without tightening until the pull of the line below the fish has made him start to move upstream, the hook hold has been in the tongue or the forward part of the mouth.

Thirdly, a decision must be made as to the advisability of striking. I have satisfied myself that on average the jerk of a positive strike does not result in as deep and firm hook-hold as does tightening smoothly and firmly. Furthermore, I have found that striking results in missing the offer completely more often than with tightening.

My main conclusion from these findings is that the best policy to be adopted for springers is not the most suitable for the other fish. When only the spring fish are in the river, there seems to be no doubt that it pays to give the salmon plenty of time, and the popular method of giving two or three yards of line before tightening is usually the safest. When the fish takes with a head-and-tail rise, which indicates that he will drop back to his lie without turning against the current, I find it most enjoyable to give lots of line and let the downstream belly hook the fish; but I do not claim that this ensures a more secure hold than tightening after giving the more customary two or three yards of line. When, however, a fish takes and there is no immediate indication that he will not turn against the current to return to his lie, I am convinced that it is safer to tighten than to rely on the downstream belly.

As soon as the small summer fish and grilse make their appearance, the problem becomes much more difficult. There is the same need as with springers, to give the fish sufficient time to ensure that its mouth is closed on the fly before attempting to hook it, but not to delay so long that the fish is given a good chance to eject the fly. Unfortunately, it cannot be said that the giving of two or three yards of line is a safe and reliable solution. According to the character of the water and general conditions, it may be that it will be quite effective on occasions, but at other times, in apparently identical circumstances, it will result in offer after offer being missed.

The method I have found to be the most consistently successful is to hold the rod-tip high, give no line at all and leave it to the salmon to hook himself against the firmly held rod. I am always ready to let the fish take line through my fingers at some tension once I sense that he is hooked, but that is simply to prevent too heavy a jar on the fine tackle when the fish is returning to his lie at speed. The straightening of the curve in the line between the rod-tip and the fish seems to result in very suitable timing and a satisfactory percentage of secure hook-holds.

A remarkable feature of this system is that on numerous occasions I have found that when the fish has failed to hook himself, an immediate repeat cast similar to the one that produced the offer has resulted in the fly being taken again and the salmon being hooked. One can seldom be sure that it is the same fish that has come again, but it certainly seems to be so.

17

This method is equally successful with spring fish, and if the angler wishes to adopt one single way of dealing with offers for the whole of the season, that alone is reliable.

Many people seem to think that different policies are required for beats or rivers of different character. If such thoughts are reviewed in the light of the behaviour comparison between springers and other kinds of fish, it will perhaps be agreed that it is the time of year that dictates the changes of method rather than the actual river being fished.

In that connection, superficially it would seem that the speed of the current should have an important influence on the length of time that the fish should be given before taking action to hook him, but in practice the variation in the tactics required to fish the fly most effectively tends to equalise the position regarding timing. In the relatively deeper steady lies which springers tend to favour, the fish usually has his mouth closed tight on the fly by the time the line reveals there has been an offer, and then it is safe to let the fish hook himself. In the faster, shallower water that offers the best opportunities with the summer salmon and grilse, the take of the fish registers much more quickly. But the tightening of the good length of line needed to work the fly properly in such water results in an adequate delay before the fish hooks himself, without the need for any line to be given. In other words, by holding the rod still and letting the fish hook himself, it usually works out automatically that the springer is given more time than the other fish.

A great difficulty in discussing in abstract such things as striking, tightening, or letting the fish hook himself, is that the physical interpretation of these words varies so much between anglers. One man's tightening could appear to be a positive strike to another. And almost invariably we anglers have involuntary habits of which we are quite unconscious. This is especially true in relation to what we do, or think that we do, when we get an offer to the fly.

It cannot be stressed too strongly, therefore, that only those who are dissatisfied with the proportion of offers that result in fish on the bank should be persuaded to make any change in the method they employ. An angler who only occasionally misses or loses a fish should leave well alone.

A certain highly accomplished ghillie on the Aberdeenshire Dee – who seldom fails to get his fish – always strikes promptly against the moderate check of an open reel when he realises that his fly has been taken. It would seem that one apparent fault corrects another, and although the thought of it makes me shudder, I agree heartily that, for him, his method is as near perfect as it could be, and that my shuddering is an impertinence.

Chapter 2

Salmon Taking Short?

When all the talk along the river is of the fish 'taking short', it usually seems that the abortive offers are much more plentiful than are the apparently more solid takes during those better times when the encounters are ended more satisfactorily.

The comparison is, of course, very deceptive. The playing of fish on good days occupies a lot of time which could otherwise perhaps produce further offers. Response from the salmon when they are thought not to be taking 'properly' is probably not really any easier to induce than when they take the fly completely into their mouths. Nevertheless, the frustrating kind of offer is a very interesting challenge.

Like most anglers closely acquainted with trout and sea-trout as well as salmon, I used to accept without question that this apparently half-hearted or overcautious kind of response was common, in fact and in principle, to all three sorts of fish. Eventually I began to think that very illogical; the factors which could reasonably be considered to explain such behaviour on the part of trout and sea-trout could not hold good for salmon.

If the species of fish that actually feed in the river – and need to do so fairly regularly – for some reason or other have not much appetite at that particular time, it is quite understandable that they could be tempted to mouth the fly and then decide that they did not really want it. Or perhaps they could just give it a suspicious nudge. But the salmon cannot lose the edge to an appetite that he has not got. It seems to me that, certainly as far as flies are concerned, it is very far-fetched to imagine that reflex action can impel him to take in an undetermined or indifferent way the object that creates the attractive illusion. When there is something about the fly that proves to be not to his liking as he approaches it, he turns away; but that is a very different matter. 'Rising short' is quite easily understandable; it offers no explanation for 'taking short'.

When the conditions of light and water are such that a salmon can be seen to move up from the depths and take the fly, his movements are so positive, so precise, that one cannot fail to think that there is practically no element of chance about it. It does give the impression that if the salmon sets off wanting the fly, and assuming that it is being fished reasonably well, he will make no mistake about getting it well into his mouth. At one time, that made me think that short takes must be purely the accidental result of bad control of the fly by the angler.

But the weight of evidence that salmon do intentionally 'take short' on occasions appeared to keep on growing, and I had to discard any idea that it was simply due to faulty fishing. Then, fortunately for my peace of mind, my experiments with variations in the ways of hooking fish threw a new light on the subject, and suggested what I consider to be a satisfactory explanation.

It was a few seasons ago in the late summer when the first of the revealing events took place. The pools contained a good mixture of grilse, summer salmon and springers which were then quite coloured. Other rods were missing fish that were said to be 'taking short', and, of course, I had my share of misses too. But I was primarily engaged in a thorough trial of the method of giving no line and leaving the fish to hook himself against the stationary rod. I was quite surprised, and, at first, thought that I was extremely lucky when I landed two or three red cocks that had been hooked in the kype. I visualised the iron being drawn from further inside the mouth and accidentally catching into the kype as it was passing. Then as time went along, I became very intrigued by the fact that many of the fish I caught were hooked in the cavity in the top jaw that accommodates the point of the kype. Evidence of that sort has since been sufficient to indicate strongly that red fish certainly, and probably others, go for the fly on occasions with the sole intention of just nipping it between the extremities of the jaw.

The tendency for the fish appearing to take short is not nearly as common in spring as it is from late summer onwards. It makes me wonder whether the salmon becomes very conscious of his rapidly growing kype, and, when he is in a very alert mood, is tempted to try it out like a child with a new toy.

Later it occurred to me that perhaps fishing the fly too slowly encouraged the fish to content themselves with nipping it only, and that a faster moving fly would induce a proper take. My trials seemed to confirm this, and now I regard the so-called short takes as positive evidence that the fly needs to be fished faster. At the same time though, a hook-hold in the kype or the corresponding cavity is extremely secure. And, in a peculiar sort of way, there is some extra satisfaction in modifying the tactics used to hook the fish instead of altering the way the fly behaves, so that even on his own terms, so to speak, the fish is still beaten.

The honour, nevertheless, goes to the salmon. If he can – as now seems certain to be the case – rise through a strong current to meet a tiny fly and pin it with the point of his kype, it is no mean feat. Presumably he will not succeed every time, but it seems that he is usually keen to have another try at the next cast when he has failed once. Even when he gets a good grip on the fly in that way, the iron is not always, of course, in a position that will ensure penetration and a hold. It would seem that a very small iron gives a better chance than a large one of the point being held in the fish's grip and of its penetrating.

My concluding thoughts on the subject are, to me, very encouraging. I am almost entirely convinced that salmon never intentionally take short in the same sense that trout and sea-trout do, and that if the salmon are responding to the fly at all, there is always some way of attempting to hook them that offers fair prospects of success. Furthermore, the ability of the salmon to rise in a strong current and give a relatively small object a good nip with his kype gives me confidence that when the fish are in a taking mood, a fly which is reasonably correctly selected and fished, will never traverse the vicinity of the lie of a salmon without gaining his notice as clearly and distinctly as is desired.

Chapter 3

A Greased-line Controversy

Some critics of the teachings of A.H.E. Wood, the originator of greased-line fishing for salmon, have expressed a remarkable opinion. His well-known methods of presenting the fly, they declare, are only really suited to the Cairnton waters of the Aberdeenshire Dee, where Wood did almost all of his fishing. They claim that those pools have peculiarities of their own (what pools have not?), and that Wood's particular techniques are seldom effective elsewhere.

This should never be allowed to go unchallenged, though the widely experienced greased-line fisher who is well able to refute it may not feel himself to be very concerned. He will probably say that you should always use the current to make the fly swim at the depth you think best while it covers the lies of the salmon at the pace dictated by you. So long as that is achieved, it does not matter whether the placing and control of the line bears the hallmark of Wood, Balfour-Kinnear, Waddington, or one of the other accredited experts. Indeed, it may well be that the most convenient way to make the fly perform as desired is a compromise between two normally distinctive styles – perhaps an improvisation of the moment, or even some personal refinement that has not yet attained adoption by a popular author.

Such an understanding would seem sound enough as far as it goes, but it does not isolate the vital point of disagreement that apparently exists between some of the experts.

Had the critics always given clear, tangible reasons for their startling verdict against the Wood methods, the problem now confronting the tyro would either not have arisen, or would have taken on an entirely different form. As the position stands however, it seems that he is expected to submit to almost blind acceptance of their extraordinary inference. And according to what some readers of

23

'Creel' say, this appears to them as a pretty wholesale condemnation of what they have so far been able to learn of the theory of greased-line fishing.

For my part, there are two strong reasons why I do not propose to try to elicit any explanation of the view that the Wood methods are seldom effective away from Cairnton. Firstly, I am convinced that nothing could be further from the truth. Secondly, the subsequent writings of that particular expert who was chiefly responsible for the myth are tantamount to a complete – but regrettably unacknowledged – withdrawal of his former allegations.

Why then should he, and those who echo his words, have ever believed that Wood's methods were so limited in their powers? I consider that one of two factors is probably the answer. Possibly they assume that the effective interest of salmon in small flies near the surface is restricted to a much narrower variation in the speed at which the fly traverses the lies of the fish than can be proved the case. Alternatively, the critics might have made a wrong assessment of the way the fly does actually behave when fished in the Wood manner. Perhaps they accepted Wood's own views about that, which, in some cases, I believe to be subject to quite a degree of error.

It will be known that the great man himself never made any claim to have finished his study of greased-line fishing, and he confessed freely that he was very uncertain about many aspects of the behaviour of salmon and their response to a small fly near the surface. I suggest that it can be seen that sometimes he did misjudge the way in which the fly was affected by the positioning and resistance of the line. He frequently referred to his liking for the fly to drift with the water like a 'dead thing', preferably showing its side view to the fish. Such action on the part of the fly is certainly a physical impossibility, because if the cast and line were not to prevent such inanimate drifting, they equally could not prevent the fly from progressive sinking, and then it would not be drifting as Wood imagined.

From this it will be seen that the argument against Wood to the effect that to have the fly drifting unchecked near the surface is not attractive to the fish, is quite void.

A summary of the matter would, then, seem to be this: the most serious difference – in fact, the only real difference – that exists

24

between the ideas of the experts is purely a question of how quickly the fly, swimming on an even keel, should be allowed to pass over the lie of a fish. And for the novice, that is a question of how squarely or obliquely he casts according to the pace of the current, and how he subsequently mends his line.

Only practical experience of any particular beat at any particular time will reveal any fine limits for suitable speeds at which to fish the fly that might be operative. The novice will probably need local advice in this respect, but at the same time, it is not uncommon for experienced rods to become much too stereotyped in their attempts at the solution.

Often it is well worthwhile to experiment with very drastic changes in the speed at which the fly covers the fish. The concentration in the early part of the season on trying to fish the fly as slowly as possible tends to make one's ideas too circumspect in the later spring and summer. Then there are many occasions on all sorts of rivers when the slow moving fly is refused, and the only effective way is to fish in the typical Wood style. Furthermore, sometimes when the surface is rough, it is more important to get the fly a bit further down than to make it fish slowly. The Wood method is the simple way to achieve that.

The novice should also remember that no matter how well he succeeds in fishing his fly, it will be at a discount if the salmon becomes too much aware of his presence. One of the most common faults is to become too static and keep on casting away in the same spot, no matter how promising it may look. Overfishing the lies in this way is terribly bad policy. It is much more profitable to move along at a regular pace, and then fish the pool down again for a second or third time.

It is understandable that for the tyro the excitement of the take and fight, and ultimately the joy of landing the fish, are a very satisfactory end in themselves. But the important thing to do at that moment is to make a point of fixing firmly in one's mind a picture of exactly how the fly was thought to be performing when the offer came. Then one has a bit of evidence to think about that is more meaningful than a whole lot of abstract theory.

As time goes along, the accumulation of such memories becomes your most invaluable guide. Some instances you will no doubt associate with the writing of one of the great authors, others with advice gleaned elsewhere. But at the beginning of a new day, it will be your decision about the speed of the fly that will count. And there will be times when I am sure you will have good reason to be glad if you choose the methods for which we owe great thanks to A.H.E. Wood.

Chapter 4

Salmon Lures – The Importance of Size and Speed

A period of elation is sure to follow the landing of the novice's 'first-ever' salmon. But usually it is not long before the historic event prompts a lot of questions. And it is remarkable how often the newcomer to the sport puts his finger on the kernel of the problem soon after his first success. 'I caught my twelve-pounder on a two inch Devon' he says. 'Why then were those rods using greased-line so fussy about the exact size of their flies when all of them were so much smaller than my bait?'

The experienced angler will always try to give his protégé an explicit answer without any avoidable complications. But inevitably he finds that whatever explanation he offers, the exceptions can seem to make nonsense of the rule. Nevertheless the task cannot be shirked. The novice must not be allowed to get the impression that the different methods of fishing lack an overall relationship. A balanced view must be established so that he will not become too prejudiced in any one direction, which may be to his future disadvantage.

It is a matter, therefore, of pressing home broad principles and showing how the apparently extreme variations in methods that sometimes account for fish are not, in fact, a denial of the main theme.

Certain assumptions must, of course, be accepted as a basis. It seems reasonable to work on the idea that all artificial lures (flies and spinners) are taken as illusions of small creatures – perhaps little fish – that arouse the predatory instincts of the salmon. In that case, the general rule can be made that the speed at which the lure may be fished successfully is limited by its size. The smaller the simulated natural creature is, the less its maximum possible speed is likely to be. The larger it is, the more quickly it may be capable of moving, but that does not mean to say that it will always go as fast as it can. This is,

27

in fact, in conformity with what happens in practice – small lures normally need to be fished slowly, while larger ones may be successful when moving appreciably faster.

At this point it is well to recognize that the selection of the size of the lure has nothing to do with any shortfall in the eyesight of the salmon. Large lures are not used because it is feared that small ones will fail to be seen. The deciding factors in choosing the size are the depth and speed at which it is known that it is the best policy to fish. Hence the large flies and baits necessary in the early part of the season in order to give a suitable performance, especially in fishing slowly enough, at the deep level where they are required to be, and the very much smaller artificials for fishing, again slowly enough, near the surface in summer. In the spring, light spinning and greased-line fishing may kill equally well at the same time: in each case success depends, as the rule suggests, on the lures being fished at suitable relative speeds.

All this, of course, is dependent on what is meant in practice by fishing the lure fast or fishing it slowly. Some of the experts would discuss this in terms of miles per hour of the water speed of the lure, as opposed to the rate at which it moves in relation to the position of the rod. But the water speed of the lure is very difficult to judge – particularly for the novice – even if a good approximation of the rate of flow of the surface water is known. Therefore an easier guide to the correct speeds at which to fish is desirable. The simplest answer is to say that with sunk-line fishing, greased-line fishing and all spinning downstream and across, any difficulty will nearly always be to fish the lure slowly enough. If the large Devon or sunk fly is not fouling the bottom, it is extremely unlikely that it will be fishing too slowly, and then the same thing applies to the sub-surface fly, so long as it is not dragging on the top.

Once the technique of fishing slowly enough in widely differing types of current has been mastered, it is very simple indeed to make the lure speed up as much as might be thought desirable. But considerably more experience will probably be needed before the top limits of speed for the lures in normal fishing can be judged confidently. In the meantime, the novice can be assured that those limits will often be reached – indeed exceeded – even when he is trying to fish as slowly as he can. Any advice he is offered while he is fishing with a view to helping him to slow down the speed of his lure should be heeded most carefully. Of course, much of the skill in successful salmon fishing lies in this appreciation of the normal top limits of the lures and at least some apprenticeship must be served before it can be attained to a reliable degree.

As indicated earlier, there are several variations of methods that perhaps seem to make a mockery of the plea to fish slowly. In a big, clear water early in the season, a long slender silver or gold wobbling spoon will sometimes take fish when moving extremely quickly compared with normal fishing speeds. But this more startling appearance and action soon loses its attraction in any one pool and then seems to put the fish completely off. Admittedly it often proves to be worth a trial when other methods have failed. But if two or three rods were sharing a limited amount of water, the fast, wobbling spoon would give them very little chance of the consistently good sport all round that is quite common with ordinary Devons and big flies. This makes it obvious that the extra speed, flash, and erratic movement create an illusion that is only on the fringe of what is most acceptable to the salmon in the way of appearance and action. Thus the broad principles that have been adopted, are confirmed rather than refuted.

A little later in the year, light spinning can be very effective when ostensibly the bait is travelling very quickly. Most experts share the view, however, that the most deadly moment is when the lure is changing direction in the current and they take pains to make this occur just in front of the salmon. The angler positions himself a little upstream of the lie of the fish, casts well upstream, retrieves rapidly so that the bait does not foul the bottom, and by watching the line and checking the speed as necessary, the bait is made momentarily to assume a side-on position in the current opposite himself and slightly upstream of the fish. It will be appreciated that at that precise time, the bait is moving relatively slowly – certainly nothing like as fast as before or after the turn. And this method is not, as it might superficially appear to be, at variance with the broad principle under discussion. Later again in the season, small summer salmon and grilse seem to prefer rather speedier lures than the springers, especially when the river is low and clear. All this amounts to, though, is reduced effort to fish very slowly, and is well in keeping the general rule.

It must now be admitted, however, that sometimes in summer a salmon will rise from its lie and intercept a spinner that passes over him at a relatively high speed, more or less directly in line with the current. Also, on rare occasions, a salmon will chase and sieze a bait, or more exceptionally a fly, while it is being retrieved rapidly simply with a view to recasting. But if it were possible to compare the total numbers of fish taken each season on lures moving rapidly and those fished at the normally accepted speeds, it would probably be the most convincing proof of all that the exceptions are no serious challenge to the rule.

Unfortunately from the standpoint of not wishing to diminish the emphasis on the importance of fishing slowly, the brief cannot be completed without it being said that the lure can, in fact, be fished too slowly. However, if this statement is considered in its full context, no harm will be done. At all times and in all conditions the salmon should be treated as if he were an exceedingly lazy fish. The best presentation of the lure at any level is such that it enables him to take it with the minimum of effort. In cases when the fish has to rise to reach the lure, a movement forward and upward closely in line with the current, and then a gentle descent back to the lie, is the least strenuous. Consequently the objective should always be that the lure should makes its appeal in time for the salmon to intercept it as near the optimum position as possible. But if the fish is given too good an opportunity to observe the lure before he must start to move to make the interception, there is a risk that he will hesitate and then do nothing. Perhaps in such cases the lure loses its illusionary quality and is then seen for nothing more than what it is, or maybe the salmon's reflexes create an insufficient urge if they need not be acted upon within a narrow limit of time. Whatever the reason, however, there is no doubt that while the salmon must see enough of the lure, he must not see too much of it.

In the cold water of the early part of the year, the salmon's reflexes appear to operate more slowly than in summer-like conditions. This permits a longer look at a bigger lure, so to speak, without the fish being put off. When the water is much warmer, just a glimpse of a tiny fly is often enough to evoke a response.

Now the two functions of the speed of the lure will be seen more clearly. Firstly, a suitable illusion must be created for the right length of time and secondly, the salmon must be given an easy chance to take the lure.

30

In abstract, this may sound terribly difficult. In practice with suitable tackle and lures for the prevailing conditions, the novice will find that he will readily make an adequate judgement of the speed required to take fish once he has achieved the line control to fish his selected lures very, very slowly indeed.

Chapter 5

Summer Salmon Problems

The extraordinary phenomenon in spring of salmon changing to a new preference for relatively small flies fished near the surface is very factual and well known. There is much evidence to show that this development is related to the rising temperature of the water. And since most anglers accept that, briefly, forty-eight degrees Fahrenheit is the crucial figure, they await a reading in that vicinity before laying aside the sunk-line in favour of the greased-line.

The sport had as a result, inadvertently created the impression that the inclination of the salmon undergoes its change very suddenly – indeed, many anglers believe that to be the case. Whether or not such an assessment is correct, it *is* true to say that this categoric alteration in the behaviour of the fish is the only one so positive that it is accepted universally. The tendency sometimes towards a reversal of the position in autumn, is much less clearly defined. And although some rods then consider sunk-line to be the more effective, others maintain their confidence in the greased-line method. Certainly it would not be untrue to say that all the salmon in the river in autumn, follow a uniform pattern of change in behaviour comparable to the springtime phenomenon.

The arrival of June, however, brings certain summertime complications that suggest that it is worthwhile taking a more critical look at the popular view that the salmon is subject only to the one basic change in what is needed to evoke its full-hearted response to a lure.

Given reasonably favourable conditions, it can be expected that the early part of the month, at least, will bring good sport up and down the country to orthodox greased-line tactics with springers, summer fish, grilse and also good sea-trout. But in most years, the way this very satisfying fishing gradually falls off, makes it appear that all migratory fish lose interest more and more as the summer progresses;

32

ultimately they are practically uncatchable with fly in a normal water in the daytime, excepting perhaps towards dusk and around dawn.

A little research has shown that these periods of 'dead' days coincide with warm close nights, when the temperature of the river changes very little over the twenty-four hours. In other words, when conditions are just right for the best sport with sea-trout during the hours of darkness, the prospects for normal greased-line fishing for salmon are at their lowest ebb. It is well worth noting, though, that the reverse also frequently holds good – if the river 'steams' towards the end of a hot day, thereby giving the warning that sea-trouting will not be much good, there will be a fair chance of the salmon taking the next morning before the water has warmed up to its full daytime temperature. And if the weather of that next day is such to keep the water a little cooler than of late, it is possible that the salmon will be responsive for a longish period, or perhaps during numerous short spells at irregular intervals. It should also be mentioned at this juncture that the salmon are often found to be in an interested mood when the atmosphere freshens up after a storm has broken, also when a strong wind starts to blow up – and equally when a gale begins to subside.

Such summertime opportunities, however, only tend to conceal one aspect of the disposition of the salmon in hot weather which is little appreciated and seldom exploited. There is abundant evidence to show that many of the days that are written off as being utterly useless could be quite productive if suitable variations in tactics were adopted; and most anglers will have had experiences which should be convincing confirmation of this. For example, days will be remembered when the only offers that came, were either after a careless mend had jerked the fly or when a sudden pull of the current on the line caused the fly to start skimming the surface. Rises of that sort usually catch one unprepared, of course, and most of them are missed. Nevertheless, the indications of the necessary changes in tactics are clearly shown.

In fast water it is easy enough to fish the fly round very quickly and practically on the surface. This accounts for many grilse and sea-trout, but it is equally effective with salmon on the right day. The popular method in North America of putting a half-hitch round the shank, just below the eye of the fly, to make it skim is also gaining adherents here; it is well worth a try.

Smooth steady water presents a more difficult problem. My own

33

favourite method is to watch a pool long enough to get familiar with the spots where the fish show, and note the direction they take after breaking the surface. Then, using the cover created by the disturbance of the surface by the fish, I cast so that I can retrieve the fly quickly and, as nearly as I can judge, in line with the path of the fish, but in the opposite direction, so that the two will pass each other. These tactics have taken salmon even in the middle of hot days in low clear water in all kinds of rivers, including spate streams.

The success of the small fly – sizes eight to twelve according to circumstances – fished quickly and on or very near the surface when more orthodox ideas seem useless – makes me think that the change in the interest of the salmon that this denotes should be recognised by anglers just as positively as the earlier one that marks the start of greased-lining. Admittedly, changes in the weather or the state of the river can bring about a return of success with normal greased-line tactics, but a similar reversal can apply in spring when a spell of unseasonably cold weather comes. Then it often pays to resume sunk-line fishing until the water warms up again.

The temperature of the water and the range of its variation over the twenty-four hours are undoubtedly the key to the problem. And certainly when summer nights remain too warm to cool the river down, the behaviour of the salmon enters a phase which is peculiar to such conditions.

Holiday anglers in particular have to cope with conditions as they find them. On some of the days when local rods do not consider it worth turning out, it could be very rewarding to keep an eye on the river. If fish are seen to be moving in such a way as to suggest repetition or regular patterns, the possibility of sport should never be ruled out.

I believe there remains much to be done in the way of finding the most suitable patterns of flies for high summer conditions. Meanwhile, there are a few rough guides that may be useful. In smooth water, in all kinds of light, a dark brown nymph-like fly on, say, a No.10 iron is usually effective; the Creel Fly is a very suitable answer. In streamy water I prefer a Blue Charm in very strong light, a Silver Blue in intermitent sunshine, and a Creel Fly in very dull conditions. At the same time though, I believe that the movement of the fly is much more important than the pattern.

A single-handed sea-trout rod is best for this kind of fishing. The finer the line and cast that can be made to do the job, the better. The salmon fight furiously without much strain being put on them. Sometimes one has to be pretty mobile to keep in reasonably close company with the fish, but the light tackle seldom fails to be adequate.

When the angler has had the experience of killing salmon with high-summer tactics, he will be subject to comments to the effect that the occasional fluky success has no real meaning. Happily, however, he will then be safely immune from the influence of the doubters.

Chapter 6

Escape Tactics for Salmon

I have a beautiful 5½lb silver grilse in the deep-freeze. It is being kept for Christmas, but that is not why I think that I shall remember this fish as clearly as any I have ever caught. And the spirited, speedy and spectacular fight he put up is only one of the very different reasons why he will not be forgotten.

A very long line was out when the grilse took the fly with a dash across the surface. He hooked himself and, without ever stopping, tore off the rest of the line and a good twenty yards of backing at a fantastic rate. His sprint was downstream and across towards my bank. Then a wild leap apparently started a change of direction, and everything went slack. I reeled in frantically, hoping that I would tighten on him again and not simply recover a vacant fly.

The suspense was very short. His next position that I became aware of was upstream of me and mid-river. My winding and his movement had made the line suddenly slash through the surface of the water in a wide whistling arc. The grilse had felt the growing strain on the line more quickly than I realised what was happening, and he showed his resentment by another wild throw out of the water.

From then on, I managed to maintain contact a little better, but I was conscious all the time that he was, indeed, making an absurdity of the thirteen-foot rod, and my pretence of being in control. But he had made a splendid job of fixing the iron in the angle of the jaw, and ultimately it was only the superior weight that brought him, still kicking and thrusting, up the gravel beach.

For my peace of mind, I was glad that I could feel less undignified about the procedure I had adopted to gain the grilse's interest. And that is the second reason why the episode will remain in my memory.

I had seen the fish rise in the same spot – towards the other bank – two or three times. Having shown him the fly twice in the normal way without result, I decided that was not how he wanted it. A fish in the mood to show freely on the surface in the manner he did can seldom resist 'escape tactics'; with that in mind, I retreated several yards upstream.

I put a long, oblique line out, and made a big mend upstream so that the fly was approximately in line with the fish, but about fifteen yards upstream. Then I let everything drift and fed a few yards of extra line. When I judged the fly was approaching a point five or six yards above the grilse, I held the line in check. There was a moment or two's wait; then came the thrilling take.

The idea was to enable the fly to sink relatively much deeper than usual, and then, by checking the line, make the fly rise through the water a little way in front of the lie of the fish. It will be appreciated that the normal escape route of any small creature that feels menaced by a predator is upwards and with the flow of water. In that way it can attain the greatest speed. I think that all game fish are keenly attracted by this action, which would seem to impose a time limit on the opportunity for capture, so to speak. Furthermore, I believe that this simulation of escape is actually created by several of the tactics used with other objectives in view.

Frequently one reads of presenting the fly broadside-on to the fish. I maintain that this can only be done by drawing the fly across the current, however slight it may be. Most of the times when it is assumed that the fly is drifting in this cross-current fashion, it must necessarily be sinking with the bend of the hook downwards, which is hardly likely to be attractive to the fish. But when the fishing-out of the cast reaches the stage of the line giving a definite draw to the fly, it then rises in the water and still moves also in the direction of the current. That, I contend, is the deadly moment, and any success is wrongly attributed to the fish seeing a side-on view of the fly.

Similarly, when a light spinning bait is cast squarely or a little upstream, the movement that attracts the fish is said to be when it is swinging round, or changing direction. But if some thought is given to this, it will be appreciated that just prior to the bait cutting against the current, it must both rise in the water and drift a little at the same time.

This action can be produced with greater positional accuracy by allowing the bait to drift a little way towards the lie of the fish without any check from the line, and then holding the bait against the current.

It is a manoeuvre that frequently succeeds when the spinner that covers the fish at an unchanging level fails.

The same movement can be exploited profitably when wet fly-fishing downstream for trout. And the grayling fisher trotting the worm will confirm how frequently a fish takes just when he starts to recover the float at the end of a swim. Observation has shown that on many such occasions, the grayling follows the drifting worm for some distance as if it were cautiously curious, but makes a grab for it the moment it starts to rise through the water.

Perhaps the greatest value of using escape tactics when fly-fishing for salmon is that the fish do not seem to be quite so fussy that the fly should not be too big. I have had the pleasure of seeing the late George Ross of the Oykel take fish in low water on a number five Blue Charm, when nines and tens were the order of the day. He, of course, could combine the equivalent of escape tactics with backing-up. But when the latter method was necessary, I was content to choose to sit and watch him rather than to find myself involuntarily seated in an unselected position, as I invariably did when I attempted any backing-up.

On the evening of the grilse, incidentally, I handed over another fish, an eleven pound salmon, to a guest rod. Considerately he suggested that he should take instead the smaller fish, for which he would be grateful, and I'm afraid he was rather set aback by my less thoughtful, three word reply.

Chapter 7

Springers and the Sunk Line

No doubt you will agree that the most highly prized kind of salmon behaviour is when the fish are responding freely in the late spring to the small subsurface fly fished on the floating line.

It can be argued very convincingly that reflex action is then the responsible factor. And that being so, it is clear that everything possible should be done to exploit to the full the element of surprise.

The angler must be careful not to be seen by the salmon so obtrusively as to detract from its possible eventual interest in the fly. And the fish must not be given too many sightings of the fly from beyond its taking range before the cast is made which will cover the lie suitably.

But the most common of the possible faults on these occasions is to use a pattern which is too clearly defined to be suitably deceptive in the particular situation. When a fleeting glimpse of a vague-looking little apparition can be sufficient to induce the wide-awake salmon to leave its lie and move upwards through some rough current to make a marvellously precise interception, it becomes obvious that the selection of the fly to be used is quite a subtle problem.

It is a matter of requiring to make just enough impact – sufficient not to fail to be noticed, but not so much as to destroy the illusory effect of the image. And it gives a great deal of satisfaction to find the solution to the problem of the immediate occasion in this respect and to be able to put forward good reasons to explain why the pattern, combined with the way it is being fished is proving to be successful.

The liveliest of taking times, however, is invariably preceded and followed by periods when the salmon vary between being barely interested and downright dour. And supposing the conditions look to be very favourable in all respects for the subsurface fly, yet a spell of careful fishing has produced no result, what do you do?

The seasoned angler may decide that it will be just a matter of time for the water temperature to rise a little, and then the position will be entirely different – hopefully exactly as wished. But neither he nor anybody else can guarantee that to the eager young fly-fisher who wants to do something positive about it there and then. So what advice should be given?

Sometimes a successful answer to the problem lies in appealing to the aggressive side of the nature of the salmon. Although a mild tempered reflex action is undoubtedly the most important feature of sport at this time of year, evidence can be found to show that when the fish are inclined to be in a dormant mood, a lure with rather more impact and fished in a rather *threatening* kind of way can have a fair chance of evoking a response which appears to be of the belligerent type.

Much experience of many rods on a country-wide basis has shown that there is seldom anything to be gained by fishing a larger fly with more impact, but still close to the surface and in accordance with normal floating-line principles. But if a fairly big tube fly is used on a sunk line and made to hover menacingly just a little way above and in front of the fish, it may well bring about the desired result. But one must be careful not to overdo this kind of presentation. If the lure is a bit too big and fished too close to the bottom, there is frequently a tendency for the salmon to move aside and let the fly go by rather than seize it.

This may be because, in these circumstances, the very low angle of sight allows the lure to get too close to the fish before it is seen and then the fish is startled. In other words, the surprise element is carried too far and there is too much impact.

Hence it will be appreciated that the selection of the lure in respect of both the size and the pattern is an interesting problem requiring all the usual factors to be taken into consideration – particularly the character of the flow, the strength of the light and the nature of the background from the viewpoint of the fish. It will also be appreciated that this is much more intricate than judging the requirements to exploit the aggressive mood of the salmon in the late autumn when the lure can hardly be too gaudy or too menacing.

There can also be difficulties in respect of the type of line to be used. The now scarce oil-dressed silk line can usually be relied upon to give the required performance without much trouble. Even in quite gentle flows – providing of course, that the fly is dressed on a plastic tube and not a metal one – the presentation can be made slowly enough and at the right depth, whereas with the plastic sinking lines, especially the fast sinking versions, it can be quite a problem to prevent the lure from going too deep.

By and large, the greater the length of the sunk line that is fished, the deeper it will go; and the shorter, the shallower it will fish. But the limits thus imposed may be too restrictive to allow the correct presentation to be achieved with the plastic sinker. A line that is short enough to prevent the lure from going too deep may mean that the cast has to be made too square for it to fish round sufficiently slowly.

It does seem that there is scope for another 'mixture', or combination of materials, in the range of plastic sinking lines. It would appear that what is required is a suitable overall specific gravity to ensure that the line will actually sink, but with a greater bulk than those currently available so that it will not cut down through the water quite so readily. Perhaps this could be done by having a thicker core and an increased amount of plastic coating to counterbalance it.

In the early season, when the salmon are lying in deep water and spinning is forbidden, the fast-sinking plastic line – especially when used as a shooting-head – will get down much better than was ever possible with the silk lines and many anglers have good reason to be extremely grateful for this. But the scenario for conventional sunk-line fishing calls for a much more delicate balance, with the presentation of the lure at varying distances above the level of the fish. And it would undoubtedly be a great help if a plastic line could be produced that would give a similar performance to that of oil-dressed silk.

There is, however, another kind of situation in the late spring when the sunk line can be very successful, and in this case the plastic sinker can score over the silk line.

Often in a big, clear water, the salmon will run ceaselessly throughout the day. Then, just about the only chance with the small sub-surface fly is to confine one's efforts to well-established good resting places (these are usually in fairly shallow water). This is because, while the fish are actually on the move, they seldom pay any attention at all to small lures. But if a tube fly of, say, one and a half inches is cast at about forty-five degrees downstream on a sinking line

41

and is then retrieved by long, fairly fast draws with the free hand, it can be made to cross a fast current quite slowly and fish at the correct depth of two or three inches down. And when the lure thus crosses the path of a travelling salmon, it may make sufficient impact to induce the fish to make a slight detour to seize it.

The rod must be held at a fairly high angle so that only a few yards of line are in the water. If there is too much submerged line, it is impossible to control the speed at which the lure crosses the flow. And it will be appreciated that if this manoeuvre were attempted with the floating line, it would be impossible to prevent the fly from skimming. The heavier the line, the better it performs in this role.

An exceedingly useful feature of this kind of fishing is that, for reasons which seem to be obvious, the salmon are nearly always hooked in the corner of the mouth. And as often as not, they hook themselves, more or less irrespective of the action which the angler may or may not take. This is a sort of bonus which can be particularly welcome during the general period when sport is more usually restricted to the use of very small flies, with all the risks thus involved.

At all times, whether fishing the floating or sunk line, the less-experienced angler should make a conscious point of judging as accurately as possible the depth at which his lure is fishing, so that when an offer comes, he will have at least a fair idea of how near the fly was to the surface or, on the other hand, how close it was to the salmon.

Overall, the results are likely to show that only in very cold water early in the season can it generally be said to be sound policy to make the presentation very close to the nose of the fish. In all other circumstances, including coloured water, it is much more effective to have the lure at a level which requires the salmon to look upwards towards it and hence see it against a background of the sky, the foliage of high trees, or a very steep hillside close to the river.

In conventional sunk-line fishing, it will often be found that the best sport comes when the fish have to rise at least two to three feet from the bottom to meet the lure. In other words, in water of five to six feet, which is the ideal depth for this class of fishing, the presentation is made roughly in the mid-water area.

At the other end of the scale, when the water is around sixty degrees Fahrenheit, small summer salmon and grilse will often rise and turn away from the very small fly at the last moment unless it is literally right in the skin of the water. This means, in fact, that as little as a half an inch can make a vital difference and shows that it is, indeed, a subject requiring careful attention.

Some twenty or so years ago there was a school of thought that claimed that the areas of interest of the salmon were either close to the bottom or within a few inches of the surface, with nothing in between requiring attention. But the modern angler with experience covering all periods of the season accepts that the taking zone of the salmon can be at any point from the bed of the river to the actual surface of the water. Admittedly this widens the problem, but it can also result in a worthwhile increase in sport.

Chapter 8

Getting to Grips with Grilse

One Saturday in July some years ago there was a lovely fly water in the Lune. Naturally the full complement of rods turned out on all the beats and it proved to be a memorable day, although not in the sense to cause a lot of rejoicing.

Our local water bailiff, the late Harry Lawson, had been on night duty and this left him free during the afternoon to give a young man some basic instruction in wet-fly fishing for brown trout. Soon the novice found that there was a good fish pulling away at him. He did as well as could be expected to follow the advice that came from Harry, but before long it became obvious that the sensible thing to do was for the old hand to take over. After some wonderful sport, Harry brought a beautiful fresh-run grilse to the net. And before the beginner's first lesson was over, there were four further encounters with grilse: two that were successful for the rod and two which ended in favour of the fish. That often happens.

Reports from most of the other beats became known that evening and during the following day. Grilse had been seen in large numbers everywhere and practically everybody had had offers – numerous ones in many cases – but very few fish indeed had been successfully landed. The general opinion was that the fish were in a very difficult frame of mind and persisted in 'taking short'.

We have all heard, of course, of similar days on the Spey and elsewhere when, in rapid succession, grilse and small summer salmon were either missed altogether or hooked and lost practically straight away. Inevitably the verdict was always the same – short takes.

The popular idea of a short take – not to be confused with a short rise, when the fish does not touch the fly – is when the swirl of the rising fish is seen and the line begins to tighten, but after moving only a short distance, it goes slack again and the fish is away.

44

It must follow that what is expected of a take that is not 'short' is that either the fish should hang on to the fly and still be there four or five seconds later when action is taken to set the hook; or alternatively, the fish should run off several yards of line against a lightly-set ratchet, and eventually be found to have hooked itself. In other words, some of the spring-time practices – whether you agree with them or not – are expected to work successfully with small, quick moving, highly alert fish in water that is relatively very warm.

When the frustrated Lunesdale anglers were confronted with the story of the events with the trout tackle, they mostly shrugged it off as a case of meaningless flukes. Attempts to convince them that the grilse should only be given enough time to close their mouths properly on the fly before the line is tightened failed to make any impression, although this drill had accounted for three grilse to my own rod during a very brief session of fishing on the Saturday in question.

I should be less perplexed by this attitude of many summer fishers on the major and medium-sized rivers if the same views were shared by a majority of the rods on the spate-streams of the west coast of Scotland. There it is an unwritten law that a Low Water Number Eight is the largest fly ever to be used for grilse, and that size only when the colour in the water is still rather dense. As soon as it begins signs of clearing, the experienced anglers are quick to change down to Nines and Tens, and as small as Twelves when the colour has finally gone. But even so, the popular practice is to raise the rod and tighten on to the fish with only a fraction of delay after the take has registered. Nothing is done in haste, of course; it is simply a case of 'leaning' against the fish, so to speak, as the line is tightening. Nevertheless it is quite surprising how often the hook-hold is in the most secure spot in the corner of the mouth. Clearly this is due to the fact that the movement of the fish seizing the fly takes it bodily some appreciable distance beyond the point of interception. That being so, what reason can there be for taking no action and allowing the fish the opportunity to spit out the fly – a thing it can do with alacrity?

There is another rather different kind of grilse story that holds an important lesson. Looking upstream from one famous bridge on the Spey there is a lovely bustling stream – just the sort that grilse seem to like the best. From the left bank one can wade out a long distance through gradually deepening water. Having reached the comfortable limit, a fairly long, square cast will place the fly into a slack-looking area close to the right bank. The ghillie tells any newcomer that the grilse tend to collect in this area of steady water and if he makes a cast as described, he is practically certain to get an offer.

When the necessary throw has been made, there tends to be a greater length of line traversing the fast, streamy water than the steadier flow. Naturally the pull of the current causes the fly to draw across the slack and then swing round in the stream at what most anglers would consider to be a very excessive speed. But often the words of the ghillie seem to be borne out; the delighted angler feels some heavy resistance and finds that he is fighting it out with a lively grilse. Perhaps it is also significant that, with the strong pull of the current on the line, the small sharp hook is made to penetrate before the fish can spit it out, but without the angler having to take any action to achieve this.

I shouldn't think for one moment that the ghillie does actually imagine that the grilse lie in the slack water. But the result of his ploy is that the angler gets his fly moving much faster across the stream than he could perhaps be persuaded to do in any other way. And there is no doubt that grilse can sometimes be deceived by sheer speed when normal tactics fail.

Yet a further story is needed to cover another important aspect of the grilse problem. A friend went with me for his first visit to the Spey. On the Monday morning I started him off in a famous pool that has a long, wide, shallowing tail; so shallow, in fact, that at the bottom end one can wade most of the way across without going above the shins. My friend fished the top, seemingly better part of the pool without success and when he reached the point where he was only ankle deep and casting into very thin water, he started to reel up. But I told him to keep on fishing right to the bottom end of the glide. I also suggested to him that among the trout and parr that were feeding on the duns that were floating down in this lower part of the pool, some of those noses that kept on popping very slightly out of the water belonged to grilse. Eventually, in fast, smooth water of not more than a foot deep, there was a lovely swirl at the fly. My friend raised his rod almost instantly and after a very gallant fight, his first Spey fish, a beautiful little grilse, was safely beached.

The kind of grilse fishing which I enjoy the most is when the water is absolutely clear and head-and-tail rises can be seen here and there. It practically amounts to stalking the fish, but you must lose no time in putting the fly in front of the grilse after the rise has been spotted. Even when the river is low and clear, the grilse tend to keep on with their unique style of running during most of the hours.

Sometimes when it is possible to keep observation of the exact track of one individual fish, and thus get a proper picture of its detailed behaviour, it becomes apparent that the grilse tends to cling to a line of travel where there is a very good rate of flow in both streams and glides; and the spots where it will linger the longest are usually those where the speed of the flow is the fastest. A grilse seems to need time to make up its mind to undertake the relatively laborious effort required to negotiate the slacker, deeper parts of the pools. And consequently, the longest rests are usually taken in the uppermost fast-water lie – probably in a glide – before the start of the steady water. Hence the value of recognizing such a spot for what it is.

A single-handed rod is often the most useful for stalking grilse. In the old days lots of lovely built-cane rods were left very much the worse for wear after coping with these remarkably strong little fish. Fortunately, modern rods in glass and carbon, or mixtures of both, designed for this kind of sport, are light enough and gentle enough, yet stand up to the dogged fights without any risk of developing sets. Naturally a model that will give a good performance with a light line – a DT6F or even lighter – is to be preferred; also, it should be suitable when in the hands of an experienced angler to fish as fine as five-pound nylon.

Single Low Water irons of sizes eight to twelve give a far better casting performance than other types and they are free from any tendency to get reversed on the leader. Also, the bodies can be dressed very slenderly, which can be invaluable. In bright weather when a black body is used to make more impact, the very light dressing is not important, but in dull conditions when one resorts to the less dense colours in order to create a more indistinct, hazy image, the single hook offers definite advantages. And despite arguments to the contrary, it has devotees in respect of its efficiency in holding fish securely among the most successful of salmon fishers.

Just as much rivercraft must be used in the approach to the grilse as in the most demanding of chalk-stream fishing for wild brown trout. And as has been said, time is probably of the essence when the rise has been seen, so here you have a nice problem – the need for great stealth at a speed faster than is required of you in any other kind of fishing.

If you make as square a cast as possible to a point no more than two yards ahead of the fish, you get the best rate of travel on the fly that is possible in the circumstances. And this ploy is often very effective indeed. You see the nose of the grilse protrude from the water just very slightly as it intercepts the fly, which is still in or very close to the surface film.

The timing then is very much the same as with big brown trout on the dry fly in a fast, smooth flow. You let the grilse get its head down again and then tighten, Due to a variety of aiding factors which then apply – the straight line to start with, the upstream movement of the fish with the fly in its mouth, and the pull of the current on the part of the line that is actually on the water – the raising of the rod produces an instant result. On a very acceptable proportion of occasions, the hook-hold will be entirely satisfactory and despite all the wild antics of the grilse, it will be landed successfully.

Chapter 9

Salmon of Summer Spates

A summer holiday on a west coast spate stream has been the beginning of many a salmon fishing career. The erstwhile trout fisher, impatiently awaiting the rain that will transform the tiny watercourse to its full glory, is certain to hear how the fish react to the varying phases of the spate.

He will probably learn that the first stages of the rising of the water – before much colour appears – offer an almost certain chance of a brief spell of hectic sport with salmon, grilse and sea-trout. But soon, when the water begins to thicken, the fish show no further interest until shortly after the spate has passed its peak. Then the falling, gradually clearing water, provides the renowned, full-blooded spate stream sport. Once that has been experienced, the memory of that little river is never likely to dim.

After the first successful spate stream adventure, the new salmon fisher probably contents himself to await his next summer holiday to renew his acquaintance with the migratory fish. Usually, though, it is only a matter of time before he is drawn to try his hand on a spring salmon river.

High water in the early part of the year will probably give him the sport he desires, but eventually he will be faced with a summer spate on such a major river. Then, remembering how his small flies attracted the fish in the considerably coloured water of the spate stream, and seeing the frequent hump-backed jumps of the running salmon and grilse, he will start fishing with unquestioning optimism. Perhaps he will get an occasional fish, but it will not take him long to realise that his spate stream lures and tactics are far from being an efficient answer to the new problem.

No matter from what source the disappointed angler seeks advice, however, he will now meet with much reserve. Compared with the confident instructions so readily given about spate stream fishing, the very non-committal views he manages to extract from people about the new situation suggests that his frustration is quite commonplace. Yet, when a fish is actually caught, it seems to be such a positive affair that there appears to be no valid reason for the offers gained to be so isolated. Against such a background one does not wish to encourage ideas that there are any infallible ways of coping with the summer spate in a tributary-fed river. Nevertheless, there is a possibility of excellent sport, and to the angler who is determined to persevere some helpful suggestions may be made.

The outlook is most favourable when some fish can certainly be seen running. It is, of course, also quite possible that the salmon will be in a taking mood when none is showing – and indeed, in such a case, prospects are probably at their very best. But when no movement can be seen it is more likely that one of several reasons – frequently excess acidity of the water – will preclude any chance of response from the fish. Running fish on the other hand, are a sure sign that there is nothing about the condition of the water to put the fish off the take. Then the problem is very simple in principle, but far from easy to solve physically. The fly must appear at the right moment within easy taking range of a salmon, and when the fish are on the move – even in big numbers – the necessary coincidence is rarely achieved.

The best policy is undoubtedly to find a good resting place. But the deepish lies of that sort which yield so well in a big clear water in the earlier part of the year are unsuitable in a summer spate. In relatively warm, coloured water, the halts of running fish are usually made in shallow water. Here there is the incidental but valuable advantage that the fish does not have to rise far to take the fly.

Knowledge of just one suitable place is invaluable. Even if it only holds one fish at a time, it will not usually be left vacant for long, and it is possible to take several salmon from the identical spot in the course of a few hours' fishing. These shallow resting places, I believe, are much more numerous than is generally thought. I think that it is well worth the effort to do a lot of exploratory fishing in the generally suitable type of water in the hope of discovering productive casts that are not commonly recognised as such. This is especially interesting because the generally known shallow taking places are usually insufficient in number to accommodate all the rods that wish to operate at any one time.

The type of shallow water with the best potential for investigation is that which is found immediately above long stretches of rough, deeper water, in which the moving fish show frequently. The deep water is usually taken at one go and offers no convenient place for a halt. Consequently, when a fish that is feeling tired finds itself in shallow water where the turbulence caused by the bed of the river creates an easy lie more or less in its path, it is a great temptation for it to rest a while. We should not be put off by the speed of the flow appearing to be too great. Running fish in summer do not favour slack water for resting; a really bustling current is quite capable of containing the place that is ideal for the needs of the fish.

It is probable that small flies – nine to twelve – were necessary just before the spate. This should not be allowed to influence the choice for fast, coloured water. The iron should be heavy enough to enable it to be fished a few inches down and it is usually best to err on the big side. A Thunder & Lightning on a double, about Number Five is as good as anything.

Getting the offer from the salmon is not, however, the end of the difficulties. It often happens that a shallow resting place can only be covered properly when the line is more nearly straight downstream than we would wish, and, needless to say, this involves a great risk of failing to hook the fish securely. The best solution I have found is to fish the longest line that is practical, keep the rod tip very high, and then simply hold firm when the fish takes. Then you must be as tough as you dare with the fish. He will probably be fairly tired, but forceful strain will make him fight the rod and the current, and a short game tussle should see him safely beached near to where he took. Handling the fish too gently tempts him to drop downstream, and once *that* business starts the odds are in favour of the salmon winning the battle.

Some anglers have more faith in spinning during a summer spate, and it must be acknowledged that this method does enable the lure to be fished correctly at greater range than with fly tackle. But too often the bait is fished much too deep in a coloured water. Salmon are seen taken on worm fished on the bottom and it is assumed that the spinner will similarly do well there. This is seldom good policy. In the first place, the spinner cannot be fished as slowly near the bottom as a worm, and therefore it is not as effective with the fish that are lazing about in deep water. Secondly, the best potential takers are the salmon that are taking a rest from running, and they are not likely to be found at the bottom of deep pools.

Basically, I believe the best spinning tactics are to keep the bait near the surface where the fish will have no difficulty in seeing it, and to concentrate on shallow water. If the angler is restricted to deep steady water he will often find that upstream spinning – still keeping the bait near the surface – provides the best sport. It is pretty certain that many of the fish caught in this way are actually engaged in running and they take the lure that meets them practically head-on – when they would not move aside to intercept it if it were swinging across the current.

Quill minnows are always worth a thorough trial during the summer spate. At times these partly translucent lures kill well when the more solid-looking wood or metal Devons are ignored. Grilse and sea-trout also seem to be partial to quills.

The summer spate is bound to include periods when there is an entire lack of response. But the condition of the water at spate time is subject to sudden changes which, although perhaps visually unde-tectable, will make all the difference. We should never acknowledge defeat, therefore, until other considerations compel us to leave the river.

Chapter 10

Keep it Slender, Keep it Single

Hairwing salmon flies using buck and/or squirrel tail have been popular for so long that it would seem almost sacrilegious to suggest that anything could be better. But take a look at say, a Logie, nearing the end of its useful life and with hardly any wing remaining and the clue to be seen is very obvious. The blue throat-hackle may well be somewhat faded, but structurally it will probably be complete and still quite sound. Needless to say, that part of the fly will almost certainly be composed of fibres of dyed cock's hackle.

Fortunately, besides lasting so much longer, wings constructed of fibres from good-quality cock capes give just as good results as hair and of course, have the additional advantage of a good and economical use for the large amount of feathers that are much too big for trout flies for which the capes were originally bought. Furthermore, hackle fibres make a smaller, neater head than bucktail. These days I even tie my 'Stoats Tails' with hackle fibre and consider them to be definitely superior.

There are many different ideas about which patterns of so-called low-water flies are most effective in different circumstances. But when it is thought best to try for a rather nebulous kind of image – in order to avoid making too vivid an impact – there is no doubt that the breaking up of both the hackles and the body into different colours is a very successful policy. Paradoxically it is also true that this is the best safeguard against the risk that the fly may make an image which is barely visible to the fish.

According to the degree of clarity of the water and the strength and direction of the light, some of the prime colours are seen much more densely than others, and it is possible for a colour to be almost undetectable against a particular background. But I should think that

53

the most learned student of this subject would be hesitant about deciding how each separate colour would be seen by the fish in any one situation: hence the advisability of opting for a good variation in the colouring.

Of course in practice there is nothing even remotely new in this multi-colour approach. Many of the famous patterns which have been continuously popular for generations have employed a considerable variety of colours. But recently there has been a tendency – quite dangerous in my opinion – to use predominantly black flies in almost all conditions, or all one single colour – red, blue, green etc. For this reason I think it is timely to remind anglers purchasing or tying their own salmon flies that numerous of the multi-coloured patterns such as the Thunder and Lightning and the Logie have proved their worth beyond any possible doubt and that in most circumstances it is better to err on the side of good contrasts or variations of colour in a pattern than to have it composed of much the same colour or shade.

In connection with this question of using contrasting colours in the body and wings etc., it is interesting to note that some of the scientists who have researched the subject of the vision of fish, have conducted experiments which show that while different colours can be recognised correctly on a regular basis, fish appear to have a relatively poor awareness or concern for shape – which is possibly of inestimable help to the fly-fisher. Consequently any fear one might have that contrasts in colour may create a seemingly disjointed-looking form can probably be safely forgotten as the fish are unlikely to have any objection. Indeed, anything which tends to work against the image having a clearly defined outline is probably a great advantage in most situations, since a degree of vagueness is probably much more deceptive.

In view of the overall impression which the foregoing may have created, it is now necessary to emphasise that there are some circumstances which call for considerable subtlety in organising the kind of image which will make sufficient impact . . . but not too much.

Everyone knows how wonderfully well the Logie does in a clearing water, especially when it is sunny or the light rather strong. And it may continue to be successful when the water is quite clear, provided the light is good. But with low, clear water in very dull weather –

when the salmon can undoubtedly see better than in any other conditions – the Logie tends to make too much impact. You see a fish move up a foot or so from its lie as if starting its journey to intercept the fly, and then drop back again.

Even with silhouette flies – Stoat's Tail, Blue Charm and so on, in sunny conditions when fish are inclined to be dazzled, it is often possible to make the impact too vivid. On this subject the late L.R.N.Grey and I exchanged a lot of correspondence and found that our separate experiences led to the same conclusions. With very small, all-black flies with silver wire tags and ribbing, the salmon would sometimes turn away if the silver was overdone – ie either the wire too thick or too many turns for the tag.

Younger anglers who may not yet have had the good fortune to fish a beautiful river well stocked with fresh fish and with all conditions favourable will not have had the chance to put such ideas as mentioned above to the test. They may be tempted to take the seemingly easy course of accepting the opposite kind of advice, such as the pattern being a minor factor compared to the problem of the size, or that any fly will do as long as it is predominantly black. Clearly, however, since subtle points about patterns were sometimes so important when there were plenty of healthy, generally free takers, those same subtleties must be even more valuable today, when the stocks of fish and the quality of the water are both so much less favourable.

After going to the trouble of tying a beautiful-looking salmon fly, it is very grieving if it loses its shape and shows signs of disintegrating after only a short spell of fishing.

In my younger days I learned from a very fine craftsman on the Aberdeenshire Dee how to construct a fly in the most secure way possible. It is fairly common practice to tie all the materials in at the tail end of the fly, hence the ugly hump or the butt to cover it up. And if this part of the body should slip slightly round the wire of the shank, the whole of the dressing is subject to disintegration.

The Scotsman started by tying in the silver or gold wire or twist near the head, putting the end of the wire adjacent to the end of the loop of the eye. And by the way, he used gossamer silk, not the stronger Naples, in order to keep the heads as neat as possible. Having secured the end of the wire with close turns of the silk, he spiralled the silk down over the wire to nearly the full intended length of the body, then wrapped closely again for the rest of the way. Now he made the three or four turns of the wire for the tag, tied in the tail – usually golden pheasant topping – and spiralled the silk back to the head. He divided the two-fold floss silk into two separate parts and used just one. Having tied in the end very neatly, he wrapped the floss thinly down the body until it reached the tag and then wrapped it back again – thinly as if he were going to use a second colour – but building up a small taper if only one colour were required.

When the second colour was used, he tied it in at the head over the first one, wrapped it thinly down for two-thirds of the length of the body, and then tapered it slightly back to the head. Now he took the wire and ribbed it up the body to the head, ensuring that at all times the wire was crossing the body at an angle of forty-five degrees, thus producing the most secure construction possible and creating a constant for the amount of ribbing on the body.

For the throat-hackle he did not wind the stem of the feather round the head because that tended to make it too thick. He took the fibre off the stem and tied it in just as he would have done with hair. Once the hackle fibre was locked with two or three turns of silk, he gave it a dab of cellulose varnish – the thin, clear variety used for trout flies – to act as cement and then made two or three more turns.

He did the same with each of the different colours of hair – hackle fibre was not used in those days – and then tied off with a very neat whip-finishing knot. He used three separate coats of black or red cellulose varnish, allowing each of the first two to dry before applying the next one in order to ensure a very solid and lasting head.

It will be appreciated that this system produces a rigid cage effect and is kept permanently in position by the strand of wire running alongside the shank for the whole length of the body. For any part of the body to twist on the shank, it would be necessary for the whole to do so, and in my experience this has never happend, even with flies after a great deal of use over several years.

I still believe resolutely in singles. They 'swim' in the flow better than any other type of fly and I am satisfied that this results in many more offers coming. (Clearly the behaviour of the fly is as important as its size and colouring.) I hook as good a proportion of the takes as anglers with doubles and trebles, if not more, and certainly do not lose a bigger proportion of fish during the fight. No doubt some people reading this will number among those who, when using bulkier types of flies and seeing the amount of response to my more slenderly dressed singles, changed over and quickly got proof that the offers do come more freely to the lightly dressed singles.

Chapter 11

Hooks – Are We Missing The Point?

When you start to consider the question of the best type of hook or fly assembly system for salmon fishing with the floating line, it comes as rather a surprise to realise how many subjects are involved, and the extent to which indirect factors can be of vital importance.

The sequence of events is, of course, that first you must get the offer, requiring a suitably deceptive image to be presented at the appropriate depth. Then you must get the initial penetration of the point or points of the hook. And to achieve the ultimate success you must have a very secure hook-hold which will withstand the final strain of beaching, tailing, netting or gaffing, all of which tend to produce the situation where the water cushion has gone and a small amount of tissue or skin has to support the greatly increased weight when the head of the fish is held above the surface of the water.

As for the image, single standard and low-water hooks have each proved their worth over the years, irrespective of how they compare with other forms, the conventional salmon fly dressings on singles can be used with absolute confidence for all occasions where there is the possibility of sport with the floating line. That does not mean to say though, that one should not strive for improvement, but I believe that such is likely to be restricted to the styles of dressings.

Doubles, trebles, the Waddington types and tube flies will all produce offers in strong currents, but equally, they all cause difficulties to varying degrees in steady flows, and here comes one of the everyday problems that are often ignored but are nevertheless very important. The disposition of boulders or rock formations on the bed of the river can cause accelerations in the speed of the current and thus create ideal lies for salmon in certain circumstances, although the flow near the surface where the fly is fishing lacks the force to keep anything but a single or a light plastic tube fly 'swimming' in the desired manner. Indeed, steady flows are often considered to be hardly worth fishing, but they can be very productive: furthermore, one can learn much more from taking a fish from a lie than by getting offers in relatively turbulent water.

Of course large numbers of offers do come to all forms of flies in regular use and it would be foolish to suggest that only the slenderly dressed singles meet with the approval of the salmon, so to speak. But that is not the point: the question is to decide which is the best in respect of creating an effective image and I don't think that many people would dispute, that overall, the single achieves that purpose the most easily and reliably.

During recent years the depth at which a sub-surface fly is fished seems to have been relegated – very wrongly, in my opinion – to a far less important position in the fishing strategy of many anglers. Some use a sink-tip line almost as a matter of course, and it is a common sight to see anglers changing from doubles or trebles to plastic tube flies simply to effect a change of pattern and without giving much thought to the difference in the fishing depth that will be caused.

In order to get a sound perspective of the question of depth, I think it is a good thing to recall the days of the greased silk line, especially before the appearance of nylon. The silkworm gut casts were of a fairly standard length of nine feet, giving a constant in that respect. And if the tip of the line started to sink, it was necessary to dry and regrease it, or put on a fresh reel and line, otherwise the whole line would be sinking and all control lost. Therefore the fully floating line was a constant. All this meant that the very popular single of those days fished at a fairly consistent depth according to the speed of the flow and the size of the fly used. It should be mentioned too that the cast always had to be fully soaked before use, thus preventing any skimming which was the equivalent to the necessary present-day practice of treating the nylon leader with a solution of Fuller's Earth and water. So if you changed to a smaller fly in the old days, it could be as much because you wanted it to fish a little nearer the surface as to effect a smaller image. After all, the fish would probably see a size ten just as easily as an eight, but the ten would fish higher. This was particularly important when grilse were about, because often success with those fish depends on having the fly practically in the surface film of the water.

59

Admittedly there were usually many more fish around during the greased-line era, but salmon fishing was much more difficult compared with the ease with which excellent water coverage can be achieved today with long carbon rods and synthetic lines, which the latter shoot a great deal better than greased silk. So, the fact that huge catches were made with the fishing depth restricted to, say, between about four inches down for the larger sizes – fours, fives and sixes – and just under the surface, or even in the surface film, for the smaller sizes down to twelves, makes one wonder why some anglers wish to get the fly deeper by using sinking tips and treble hooks. If fishing at a greater depth than was the general practice in the old days had proved to be advantageous, we should surely have heard all about it and the fully floating line would have become very unpopular. But I know of no evidence of that kind and I do not think that the case for fishing deeper has been proved – certainly not on the haphazard basis of paying no real attention to the question.

Needless to say, flies dressed on singles fish practically automatically at the depth wished and present no problem. Even in heavy glides, the long carbon rod can be swung round that bit faster and thus allow the fly to sink a little more so that the single will fish at the required depth. It is also possible to organise a selection of plastic tube flies that will fish at controlled depths from the surface film down to about four inches. But with doubles, trebles and the Waddington type it is not possible always to be able to fish at the right depth and speed and their limitations in this respect must be recognized.

On the score of depth, then, the single must be voted the winner with the tube fly the second.

Now comes the most complicated and seemingly contradictory problem – the type of hook best able to ensure the successful landing of the salmon. In most situations, with the notable exception of the corner of the mouth, doubles and trebles are incapable of getting a deep penetration and hold. It has to be remembered, of course, that the hook can only be pulled in by the leader – it cannot be pushed in.

If you take a piece of foam and lay the hooks out as in Figures 1 and 2, you will see that the hooking gape, so to speak, of the double and treble is greatly reduced, and even if it were possible to sink the hook to the extent of the shank lying against the surface of the foam, the double and treble, as in Fig. 4 would still give a much less deeper hold than the single.

In practice, of course, the greatest depth to which the hook can be pulled is when the furthest point of the bend from the eye to the hook is reached, as in Fig. 3.

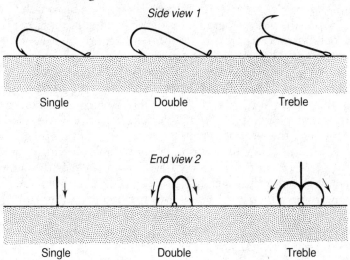

Side view 1

Single   Double   Treble

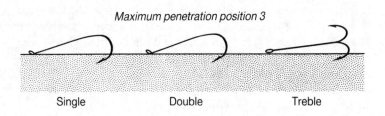

End view 2

Single   Double   Treble

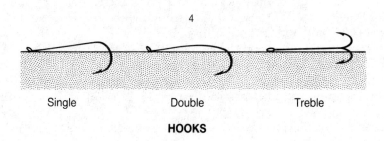

Maximum penetration position 3

Single   Double   Treble

4

Single   Double   Treble

HOOKS

It would require a push at the end of the shank to get the single deeper, and with the double and treble even that would not work, as will be seen shortly.

With the single there is nothing to stop the pull on the hook achieving this maximum penetration to the furthest point of the bend. And it will be appreciated that this process requires the shank of the hook to move in the same plane as the bend and the point, as indicated by the arrows in Fig. 2. Obviously the same thing would apply to the double and the treble, but that would require the bend of each of the two legs to cut through the skin and tissue, which cannot be done with a pull on the eye of the hook. It cannot be disputed that the single gives the cleanest, deepest penetration, but there is another factor – common also to the double and treble – which must be considered. Some hooks have very long points and barbs, and it is possible for the point to reach bone before the barb is safely buried in the softer tissue, which gives a very insecure hold. Another fault is that in some hooks, particularly the Limerick, the deepest part of the bend is too close to the line of the point and barb and this greatly restricts the depth to which the hook can penetrate.

Although I don't pretend to know what it is, there must be an optimum size of hook that will hold a salmon safely. Clearly the very small trebles that are used with the smaller tube flies and the Waddington type only get a very shallow skin hold unless they are hooked in the corner of the mouth – which is another problem to be dealt with later. Also very large hooks of all sorts with big barbs are only likely to get a skin hold which will easily scrape out. I should imagine that a Redditch size eight is in the vicinity of being the best, but I think it should have a round bend to give the deepest penetration. The standard salmon, Low Water salmon and Wilson salmon hooks, all made by Partridge, are all very good and have stood the test of time, but even so, I think the round bend and small point and barb of the Captain Hamilton Hooks, in strong enough wire and with a loop eye would be better, especially for summer salmon and grilse.

Most of the doubles and trebles tend to be of the Limerick bend or similar and that is probably as well because the round bend should not result in deeper penetration and the straighter shape of the Limerick from the point to the start of the bend is good for the initial penetration.

One use of the treble hook – spinning with a Devon minnow –

gives an unduly good and misleading impression. The proportion of offers that are successfully hooked and landed is probably the highest of any form of salmon fishing with artificial lures. But this is much more due to the influence of the Devon shell than the character of the hook. When a salmon takes a fly or bait, it gets a very firm grip on it. Think of how a golden sprat or prawn gets mutilated with just a quick pull. The grip of the fish on the Devon shell often prevents the points of the treble coming into contact with the roof of the mouth or tongue. The angler tightens and keeps pressure on. Feeling this, the salmon begins to release its grip, thus allowing the Devon to slide across and out of the corner of the mouth, where one or more of the points of the treble penetrate and give a very secure hold. But without the Devon shell to prevent the points making contact with the roof of the mouth or the tongue, the double or treble is prone to get a shallow, insecure hold inside the mouth. With the single – which must often lie flat on the tongue after the fish has taken – there is a lot better chance of the hook reaching the corner of the mouth before penetrating when the angler takes action to set the hook.

The late Eric Horsfall Turner made a habit, when playing a salmon, of giving a pretty hefty tug against the fish the first time it started to move directly away from him. He considered that if there was a poor hook-hold, this gave him a good chance of dislodging it and getting a much more secure one in the corner of the mouth. If that failed, he argued, it was better to lose the fish straight away rather than after a lengthy fight.

On the subject of single versus doubles and trebles, the late Ralph R.Whitaker, big-game fisher and expert with the 600lb bluefin tuna off the Florida Keys, would not use doubles or trebles except when spinning with Devon minnows. He argued strongly that with two legs of a hook embedded, each acted as a pivot for the other to be worked loose. And it is a notable fact that big-game fishers use single hooks.

Now the human element must be considered. Doubles and trebles do have more points capable of giving the initial penetration. And if the angler habitually fishes with his rod parallel to the surface of the water and allows the taking salmon to pull against the check of an open reel – a practice which I disapprove of strongly – he will almost certainly hook more fish with doubles and trebles than with singles. Whether or not he will land more than if he were to use singles is another matter. But any idea that doubles and trebles give very reliable hook-holds gets exploded every day on many rivers. On the other hand, if the rod is held high – forty-five to sixty degrees – and the salmon is given the appropriate time-lag according to the period of the season and prevailing conditions before the angler 'leans' against the fish to set the hook, not only is there a far better chance of the single hook reaching the corner of the mouth before getting a hold, but it will probably get a deeper and more secure hold than a double or treble if the penetration is elsewhere.

The final point in favour of the single is that it is almost impossible for it to get caught up so that it fishes in the reversed position. The treble of a tube fly often does foul the leader in windy weather and although that may not prevent a salmon taking, the chances of a reversed hook getting a hold are just about nil. Also some patterns of doubles and trebles fished without tubes allow the nylon to get wedged in a narrow space between the legs and then the fly fishes the wrong way round. This can also cause the nylon to neck and weaken.

No angler with much experience of fly-fishing for salmon will say that losing fish is not an ever present risk whatever type of fly is used. And if the individual can get the initial hook-hold on all but the occasional fish that takes, and then proceeds to land about seven out of ten of those he plays, he should leave well alone and continue with his methods and choice of hooks on one proviso, which is that he does as well or better than other rods in the same fishing circumstances. But anyone who is dissatisfied with his average performance should not ignore the use of single hooks and the practice of holding the rod high so that the fish does not feel the resistance of the rod as soon as it takes. Then all options are open to tighten as soon or late as he chooses and he will be sure to find that a lot of his fish are hooked securely in the corner of the mouth.

'Reg's River' – the Lune at Newton. *(Michael Prichard)*

Bernard Venables watching R.V. Righyni playing an Avon salmon.

Summer salmon fishing on a Scottish water.

Dermot Wilson fishes the Tamar for salmon, near Endsleigh. *(Dermot Wilson)*

Brian Harris, ex-editor of *Angling* magazine into a fish on the Lune at Newton. *(Michael Prichard)*

Reg fly-fishing for salmon on the Millstream pool of the Tweed at Upper Hendersyde in October. *(Arthur Oglesby)*

As always, Reg hardly fished when a guest arrived, preferring to watch and give a little advice, and then weigh the fish. *(Michael Prichard)*

R.V. Righyni at his fly-tying bench. *(Michael Prichard)*

The Roll Cast.

'Our imaginary river'.

Sea-trout fishing on the River Lune in Lancashire. *(Michael Prichard)*

Dry-fly fishing on the River Itchen in Hampshire. *(J.B. Lloyd)*

Fly-fishing on the River Anton, a tributary of the River Test. *(J.B. Lloyd)*

Reg and Bernard Venables trout fishing on the River Kennet. *(Michael Prichard)*

Fly-fishing on the River Anton, a tributary of the River Test. *(J.B. Lloyd)*

Reg and Bernard Venables with a trout caught at Hungerford on the River Kennet. *(Michael Prichard)*

Reg Righyni nets a Lune trout, hooked on a wet fly. Lune fish average over a pound. *(Dermot Wilson)*

Winter grayling on the fly. River Wharfe. *(J.B. Lloyd)*

An autumn grayling. River Wylye in Wiltshire. *(J.B. Lloyd)*

Grayling fishing on the River Anton, a tributary of the Hampshire Test.
(J.B. Lloyd)

Grayling and the 'Righyni' grayling-float. (*J.B. Lloyd*)

Casting with a centre-pin reel.

Chapter 12

A New Salmon Fly?

Spasmodic glimpses of the sun between grey clouds and a gently falling water, slightly tinged with colour, are good cause for salmon fishing hopes to run high. Then, with pleasurable confidence, on goes a Logie.

A variety of patterns will give a good account of themselves in those conditions, of course, and one's personal fancies can be indulged without too much risk of failing to interest the fish. But those anglers who mount the Logie do so in the belief that whether or not any other fly is as good, it is certain that none is better.

A little more, or less, brightness in the sky, or a gradual clearing of the water, do not make much difference: the Logie continues to give gratifying service. And provided only that a good flow of water is maintained, a further change to a clear river and the difficulty of a completely overcast sky will still find this splendid fly doing better than most others.

The need to have some sort of limitation in the range of patterns carried – and the problem of finding something better – are perhaps good reasons for continuing to prefer the Logie even when the water is low and clear and the light extremely poor. It is then, of course, that the angler gets the minimum of help in his efforts to create a deceiving illusion with his fly. And it is really making an unfair demand of the Logie to expect its appeal to the fish to continue undiminished.

The fact is indeed that the Logie makes a suitable impression in other conditions when the vision of the salmon is at a comparative disadvantage. And that, surely, is an indication that its impact is in danger of being *too* great when the fish is best able to see the intimate details of the fly.

Those thoughts, and my affection for the Logie, initiated my attempt, some time ago, to devise a modification in the dressing.

This had the objective of extending its effectiveness to cover the combination of circumstances in which it was too showy in its orthodox form.

The effective variation of the Logie does not amount to much more, basically, than the replacement of the silver wire and blue throat-hackle by gold wire and red-brown hackle. But the confident way in which the salmon respond to this fly in conditions judged to be the most favourable for their vision convinces me that the seemingly slight change is quite vital. And it suggests a line of thought that could perhaps be useful applied to numerous other patterns.

The blue throat-hackle and silver wire are common to several of the most killing greased-line flies. It is a safe assumption that those items are very penetrating. It may be accepted that they are a valuable asset when the state of the water, or the quality of the light, makes it at all difficult for the fly to make sufficient impact, to attract the interested notice of the fish. It follows that when the salmon can see the fly easily and distinctly, the blue and the silver are too startling, and should be avoided. In those circumstances, colours approximating more nearly to the general tone of the background of the fly seem to be more capable of creating a suitable illusion.

Perhaps that will sound merely to be a repetition of the familiar 'a bright fly on a bright day and a dull fly on a dull day'. But this adage makes no qualification about the state of the water, and consequently, the degree to which the vision of the salmon is able to function is not properly considered.

If the river is carrying a fair amount of colour on a dull day, few would dispute that the Thunder and Lightning is as reliable as any fly. And that dressing, although not bright, could not be described as being dull. The black of the body is very penetrating, and that is just as useful when the vision of the fish is impaired by a good deal of colour in the water as it is, in other flies, when strong light tends to be dazzling.

Although the variation of the Logie developed into a new fly as far as I am concerned, it now seems unlikely that such a useful pattern has not been tried before. I should be very interested to know if it is in use elsewhere, and, in such a case, how it is rated.

Meanwhile, the proud record of the Logie is such that it would be an indignity to refer to a 'Logie Variation'. Therefore, for the want of a better name hitherto, I have called it simply my 'variation'. Now, more permanently, I christen it the Creel Fly.

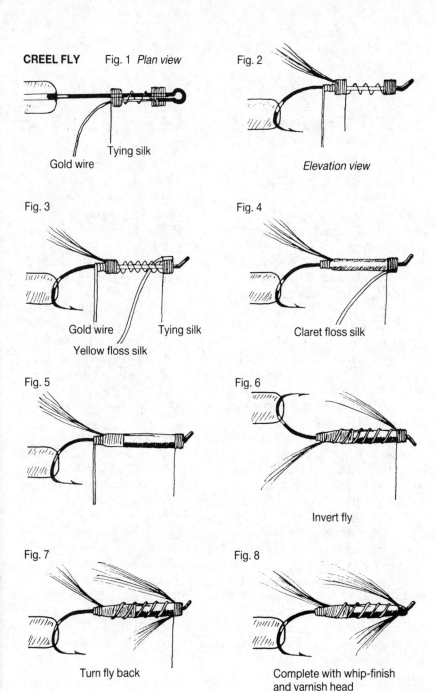

CREEL FLY Fig. 1 *Plan view*

Tying silk

Gold wire

Fig. 2

Elevation view

Fig. 3

Gold wire   Tying silk

Yellow floss silk

Fig. 4

Claret floss silk

Fig. 5

Fig. 6

Invert fly

Fig. 7

Turn fly back

Fig. 8

Complete with whip-finish
and varnish head

Chapter 13

In the Wake of a Flood

How do the pools look this year on the salmon river you fish? The tremendous floods of November are certain to have had some significant effects, both for the better and for the worse. In the early days of the season the task of becoming familiar with the changes that have taken place during the winter can always be very rewarding. This time it promises to be particularly so.

Drastic alterations may have created entirely new features in the nature of the flow in some pools – or perhaps altogether new fishable places in areas that used to be worthless. Such obvious situations present a fairly straightforward problem for investigation. But no single cast can be depended upon to fish exactly as it did towards the end of last season, no matter how reassuring the surface of the water may appear to be. And it is the more subtle changes that are potentially the most deceptive.

The distinctly new current formations pose a fascinating exercise in estimating where the salmon lies are now likely to be, and then seeing how the results of practical fishing compare. And, this being a highly topical subject early in the season, it is usually not long before all concerned have acquainted themselves with the necessary information about any such newly established 'taking places'.

Misjudgements of the situation are more likely to occur where the lies of the fish have simply been displaced to a seemingly negligible extent. Variations of this kind are frequently caused by small movements of gravel beds in relation to more permanent features, such as rocks and large boulders. And if surface indications are not suggestive of any marked change, there is a tendency for the angler who was very conversant with the old lie to cover that position much too narrowly and neglect water very close to it. Thus he may fail to discover what is now the deadly spot.

The possibility calls for the careful re-exploration of every part of the pool as if it could hold a fish, although superficial appearances suggest that time spent in that way could safely be saved. Then, besides the prospect of revealing any new secrets of the pool, there is a chance of finding long-standing lies that have been previously overlooked. Where a good inspection is not possible the less experienced angler will perhaps find difficulty in visualising what has happened to the bed of the river as a result of the floods. Some indications of the general tendencies that apply to various types of river courses may, therefore, be helpful.

In some cases the November floods spread over the river-side fields at various points. In the vicinity of estuaries, of course, the sheer volume of water and the flow of the tide against it would be responsible. But up above this low-lying land, any overflowing of the bank is usually caused by some constriction immediately below the inundated zone, such as a narrow gorge through a ridge of higher ground. Consequently, the amount of water that is able to drain away through the restricted channel is provided by the smooth surface flow of the flooded area. In those circumstances, the current at the level of the normal bed of the river beneath the vast accumulation of water is reduced to negligible movement. At this stage there is no scouring or erosive action, but shingle beds were certain to have been set in motion during the rapid rise of the water, and the down-drift of pebbles continues from the point where the river is more or less contained by the banks. The result is a tendency for the pebbles to be deposited in places where they would normally be swept aside, and the depressions in the bed of the river get filled in. The same sort of deterioration can occur to a minor degree in some places where the banks are very high and the water does not overflow them. But pools so affected are usually long and deep, and would be inclined to be rather characterless before the flood. Therefore the damage done is relatively slight and perhaps hardly noticeable.

Striking new features sometimes appear in the area that has been flooded as a result of what could be termed casualties. The falling of a tree, the collapse of a high eroded bank, the breaking away of part of a large rock, or the removal of a large boulder, can all cause pleasing or disappointing new developments. But the greatest change is likely to occur if, for some reason, the water held back in the fields while the flood subsides, finds a new gap to re-enter the river. Then it is nearly certain that a new deep hole will be washed out, and not far away, a new shingle bed will be formed. Sometimes an event of nature creates an entirely new pool.

Stretches of the river where the flood is carried by the sheer speed of the movement of the water without overflowing are unlikely to suffer a great deal from the fishing point of view. Changes are sure to take place of course, but the scouring action of the water is maintained, and therefore there is a better chance of improvements eventuating than lies being spoilt. No matter how the November floods left their mark, however, the salmon will still find lies to their liking in some of the pools: and finding the places in which to get on to terms with the springers again is a delightful prospect.

Chapter 14

Mr. Murray and Reg

For generations salmon fishers have had clear-cut, if not definitive, policies concerning the selection of patterns of flies for use with the floating line. Indeed, before the introduction of 'greased-line' fishing by the great A.H.E.Wood, some of the patterns he popularised had already gained fine reputations for certain conditions. As early as 1895 Kelson wrote in his book *The Salmon Fly* that the Logie was 'An excellent summer pattern in dull weather on the Dee', and of the Thunder & Lightning he said, 'This fly is exceedingly popular and has a well earned reputation for its destructive qualities at a time when rivers begin to rise after rain'.

But this whole problem has become a very sensitive question. One or two modern writers have expressed the view with maximum force that it simply amounts to dogmatism to attempt to rationalise on the subject. They base their argument on the fact that only a few exceptional patterns, such as the Shrimp Fly, were ever attempted to simulate or caricature living creatures. All the rest are the result of purely imaginative variations and modifications of the feathered lures that were used in the earliest days of salmon fly-fishing, when it was largely assumed that such contraptions were taken by salmon in mistake for natural food in just the same way as with trout.

Of course I agree that it is nonsense to start with a theory and then try to make events fall in line with it. But it is a very different matter to collect a lot of well-established and authenticated data, then evolve a theory in conformity with any regular patterns which emerge from the study of the details. When that principle is followed it produces a policy for the selection of the salmon fly to suit the situation which gives one confidence based on reason, instead of confusion which can easily arise from having no clear principles or ideas to follow.

In my early days I soon gained strong beliefs in certain patterns for certain conditions from both my reading and first-hand advice from successful anglers, all of which, in turn, was confirmed by my own experience.

Then I had one of my strokes of enormously good luck. I took a rod on a beat in the middle reaches of the Aberdeenshire Dee. The head ghillie had a vast knowledge of salmon and of the ideas and methods of a large number of the most successful Dee fishermen. And the best part of it was that he loved to conduct experiments and trials, just as I did. It was a case of 'Mr. Murray' and Reg, and we got along together so well that he chose to ghillie for me personally on all my subsequent trips to the beat until he retired. It was a great help, of course, that most other rods wanted to be fishing all the time themselves, while I virtually shared my rod with my highly esteemed companion.

For the sake of those who are not familiar with the Dee it should be first explained that often the water is so clear and the bed of the river so favourable that it is possible to watch the salmon in their lies and note in detail their reactions to the approach of the artificial fly. Mr. Murray and I took it in turns to do the casting and to lie on the bank opposite the salmon and observe and report.

Before giving examples of the very revealing experiments we made together, an over-riding factor should be mentioned. It is not sufficient simply to find a pattern that the salmon will take. The full requirement is that it should be a pattern that can be used in the largest size that the fish will take in the particular conditions, so that the most secure hook-hold possible can be achieved. In this same context the amount of dressing in relation to the hook size should be specified, because of the great diversification which has developed in this respect. On one occasion a friend of mine reported from a beat on the Spey in April when the water was rather low, that the fish were 'already down to size nines and would not look at anything bigger'. Eventually I was shown the size nines in question. The amount and length of the dressing was about the same as I put on my size fives.

The extremely short, small dressings of the A.H.E. Wood era – based on the idea of getting the hook-point as far as possible into the mouth of the fish – are no longer thought to be suitable, although for my own part I should prefer them to the grossly over-dressed examples which result in the hook size being much smaller than necessary. The proportions I favour – which may be slightly smaller

72

than the average shop-bought fly – are that the tag should finish a little way short of opposite the point of the hook, the tail should sweep up in a curve and the end should be a little short of being opposite the bend of the hook. The wing should end a little short of the end of the tail, and the throat hackle should be the same length or a little shorter than the body. I find this balance very successful in all respects.

The depth at which a fly fishes is also very important, but that problem is suitably cared for if one sticks to low-water irons dressed reasonably in line with the above proportions.

Now for the experiments with my very capable accomplice. One of us would settle opposite the lie of the fish. We preferred there not to be more than three fish side by side so that there was not too much distraction in the way of jostling for the prime position. The ideal situation was when there were several individual fish spread out in an irregular line downstream of each other so that the reaction of each fish in turn could be observed.

The one taking the turn with the rod started casting so that the fly would cross the stream for the first time about twenty yards above the leading fish, and then take three full paces between each cast as standard practice.

A significant fact to be noted was when the salmon gave the first indication that it had detected the presence of the fly. The relevant action is difficult to describe, but it is as if the fish freezes for a moment and then for a short spell does everything that it was doing previously noticeably faster. However, once seen, this tell-tale that the fly has made its initial impact on the fish is unmistakable henceforth.

When the fly makes too big and dense an image for the situation, the fish will notice it at fully the twenty yards starting range. Whenever we suspected that such might be the case, we first threw in a few bits of stick about the length of the fly in use and let them drift down. This never seemed to cause any concern among the fish. But the fly working across the current in the agitated manner caused by the restriction of its movement and the grain of the current was often clearly detected by the fish at that distance, even in fairly rough water.

Eventually we reached the conclusion that the most suitable distance for the fly first to be detected by the fish was when it was not more than three casts – about nine yards – upstream of the taking range of the fish. Our trials suggested that if the fly was detected at a greater distance, the fish had lost interest in it by the time it was crossing the stream within taking range. (This does not apply to the late season when salmon are in an aggressive mood.)

The vital factor was what happened when the fly was working its way in front of the fish and within reasonable taking range – say about two to three yards upstream. Sometimes the observer would yell out that the salmon had lifted in the water a little and moved forward towards the fly for a little distance, perhaps a foot or so, and then dropped back to its lie. That we took to be the sign that the fly was too big, or the image too dense, to create a fully deceptive illusion. Bearing in mind the point of wishing to use the largest fly the fish would accept, the first change we made was to a less dense pattern of the same size, say a number seven Logie instead of a number seven Blue Charm. About ten minutes later after the change of the fly and re-treating the leader with Fuller's Earth paste, also moving quietly back upstream to four casts away from the fish, operations were restarted.

Sometimes when the changed fly was within taking range, the fish would move towards it again and continue decidedly further than on the first occasion, but would then still drop back to the lie again. The drill would be followed again, but this time with a change down in size, and then often enough the fish would come all the way and take very solidly.

In those days I was also fortunate enough to have a friend, Johnnie Wilson, of Bradford, who sadly died much too young. He joined me in the same kind of experiments on the Lune, the Border Esk, etc and I acquired absolute confidence in the policy of fly selection based on the density of image required to enable the largest size of fly to be used in the particular circumstances. Briefly, it is as follows.

> Bright weather, clear water – silhouette fly – example,
> Blue Charm.
> Dull weather, clear water, or bright weather and slight
> colour in the water – normal image – example, Logie.
> Coloured water – silhouette/normal image – example,
> Thunder & Lightning.

It will be appreciated that without question such a system is in full conformity with the long-standing beliefs of many successful anglers in respect of the circumstances in which they have found certain

74

patterns to be most effective.

A very important question which arises from the foregoing is how often when one cannot see the fish do they come up a little way towards the fly and then drop back again, indicating that it has failed to make the final deception?

There was an occasion just a few seasons ago when Barry Lloyd and I were fishing together for sea-trout on the Lune. The river was clear and it was a dull evening, but there was that quality of light that enables you to see into the depths much better than is normally the case. Barry was beneath a high bank and fishing a team of three standard patterns on a floating line. He called to me and I approached to find out what was going on. Barry was quite excited. He could not actually see any fish on the bottom, but each time his flies went round several good sea-trout became visible by lifting a foot or so and then dropping back to the bottom again. Barry did change his flies, but by then the fish knew too much and could not be tempted.

It is true that if the abortive reaction of the salmon to your fly goes unseen, it is not a position that is susceptible to correction. But if, in the first place, you have taken careful stock of all the conditions and put on a 'safe' fly for the situation as you see it, there is a far better chance of success than when the choice of pattern has been a purely random affair.

And the analysis of the catches made by several rods on a good day will often give very convincing confirmation that the pattern of fly does indeed matter a great deal – that is, of course, in terms of the density of image it creates.

The sometimes scornful remarks of some fishermen have no edge whatever when you enjoy confidence in your policy and get a good share of the sport that is going.

Chapter 15

How Long is a Salmon Rod?

In considering the optimum length of a salmon fly-rod, it is essential to recognise that two different problems are involved, each of genuine basic importance.

The first is personal preference and physical adaptability. If the individual has a top or bottom limit to the length of double-handed fly-rod that he can use efficiently, it is essential that he should be fully aware of the fact and that it should be observed most carefully.

The second consideration is the question of the suitability of the length of the rod for different fishing needs, but as this is the simpler of the two, let me deal with it first.

Assuming that the rods under consideration have been properly designed and constructed from the most suitable top-quality materials, certain guidelines are quite incontrovertible.

The longer the rod you can handle efficiently and comfortably, the greater the length of line you can lift from the water, throw into a good clean back-cast, and then deliver, including the shooting of a good amount of extra line. Compared with the use of a shorter rod, this saves a lot of time and probably reduces the overall physical energy you have to expend in a day's fishing.

The longer the rod, too, the better you can execute the switch casts and all the variants of the roll-cast, including the true single and double-Spey casts.

The up-to-date version of the Spey cast – which for the average angler is possible only with a top class carbon-fibre rod – extends the line fully in the air and drops it on the water as gently as the best overhead cast. The same degree of accuracy may not be attainable, but the Spey cast need not be the splashy affair that it used to be.

The longer the rod, the better you can control the line on the water and the behaviour of the fly as you fish out the cast. Remarkably enough, this is often more important on small rivers than large. On a fast, narrow river, you often need to fish the lies on the far side of the spine of the current. Here the extra reach of the big rod is a help, while it is also better for mending the line cleanly and effectively.

On large rivers, where the longest cast often drops the fly short of the line of the fastest flow, a long rod will frequently fish all the way round perfectly and without any need for mending. In such a circumstance the shorter rod may be capable of doing much the same work as the longer one, and it is this sort of situation that makes some anglers assert that there is no advantage in having a longer rod.

Next comes the question of playing a big, lively salmon.

The other side of the river often seems to have a strong appeal to a hooked fish, and when you have all your fly-line out, and perhaps a lot of backing, the longer rod offers you a much better chance of holding enough of the line clear of the water to avoid having too much line submerged. Once a salmon is in the position of having a long length of sunk line acting as an anchor against which it can pull, the odds are tilted considerably in its favour.

The longer rod can also be a great help to the angler where bankside bushes have to be traversed by the line. It is quite gratifying to find how an extra foot or so of rod length can make all the difference and enable you to lift the line safely over such obstacles.

If the shorter rod will do your day's fishing efficiently, and without you having to strain to reach the necessary distances, any extra length, and weight, are clearly of no advantage. It is all a question of finding the correct balance.

On heavily-wooded stretches, problems can be encountered with longer rods, especially when you are playing a fish. Nothing is more galling than to be in the final stages of subduing a strong salmon and then suddenly to find that your rod-tip has touched an overhead branch and your line has become hopelessly entangled. It is well to be familiar with the greatest length of rod that the beat will take without any undue risks.

Now for the complex problem of finding the optimum length of rod for the individual, but specifically from the performance point of view and, for the moment, ignoring the question of the circumstances on the beat where the angler may wish to fish.

It seems often to be the case that if a person can perform enjoyably and efficiently with a twelve-footer, he finds difficulty with a fifteen foot rod, while those people who feel at home with the longer of the two are ill-at-ease with the shorter rod.

The temptation is to think that this is all a question of timing, but these days, with highly-efficient carbon rods, this is simply not true. Indeed, one of the most valuable features of proper design in carbon is that the rod takes its timing from you. You do not have to keep within a narrow band of permissible timings, which fact can be proved quite conclusively with the greatest of ease.

It is clear, then, that any trouble an angler encounters with a rod different in length from the one he handles best must be due to basic casting errors. These may not be serious faults, but they cause enough disruption to make the good, sensitive fisher feel that he is making a mess of his casting.

A little coaching should quickly remove the problem and the angler ought to accept without any worry that if he can cast well with any one length of double-handed fly-rod, there is no reason why he should not do just as well relatively with any other length, provided it is not too heavy.

The next question concerns the individual's natural aptitudes. Some energetic people do their best only when they are putting a fair lot of effort into their casting. Others find a comparatively leisurely approach much more to their taste.

Naturally, fast-action rods suit energetic anglers best, while steadier movers get the best results from slower-action rods. But in this context it is often the length of the rod that is the key factor. If, say, an energetic man finds that he can not get on with a fifteen foot rod, he may well find that a shorter model will suit him perfectly. The reason is, of course, that for the same speed of arm movements, the tip of the longer rod moves far more quickly than that of the shorter one. And the shorter rod sends the line out fully as quickly as is required for the class of casting involved, thus freeing the angler from the problems created by having the line move at excessive speed.

By the same token, the leisurely caster, with the shorter rod, may have his rod-tip moving too slowly to keep his line high enough in the air. Increasing the length of the rod should cure this problem automatically, simply because of the increased speed of the tip of the rod.

When everything is taken into consideration, there can be little doubt that the safest compromise is to select the longest possible rod that you can handle happily and efficiently, but will not be too long for the restrictions which may exist on the water where you are likely to do most of your fishing. And never let anyone put you off using a long rod on a little river unless there is the risk of difficulty with trees when playing fish.

Today, it is no exaggeration to say that the norm for length is the fifteen-footer. Only rods of greater length are considered to be 'long rods'. And keeping in mind the question of the long-term satisfaction with one's choice of length, there should be very sound reasons for selecting a rod that is shorter than fifteen feet.

Chapter 16

Playing a Salmon on a
Long Carbon Rod

Some salmon fishers appear to have got the impression that they used to be able to kill fish more quickly with their relatively short cane fly-rods than with the modern long carbon models of sixteen and a half or seventeen and a half feet.

Naturally, they find this to be very confusing, because they are quite delighted with the performance of their carbon rods in all other respects – ease of handling, casting very long distances with heavy lines, control of the fly when fishing it round etc.

So why should such a rod be lacking in strength when it comes to playing a salmon? The plain fact is of course, that this is a totally wrong notion. Indeed, it has the strength and capability to play a salmon to a standstill with the utmost efficiency – much better than any kind of rod in the past.

Emphasis should, however, be put on the word 'play'. The long carbon rod could be made to drag out a salmon unceremoniously as soon as it was hooked – provided the leader was strong enough – in the same way as was sometimes done with the very heavy cane and wood rods in the past. But during a sporting contest with a hooked salmon on a normal strength leader, the greater recovery rate of carbon ensures that the pressure need never be relaxed for a fraction of a moment and this has the effect of tiring the fish out without any waste of time.

And so that this assertion of greater efficiency can clearly be seen to be true, let us follow through a detailed breakdown of the ways in which the rod should be made to function when coping with the many and varied antics of the fighting salmon – sudden mad rushes, violent jerks, hurtling leaps, dogged resistance when seemingly sulking on the bottom and so on.

Firstly, when it is wished to obtain the full benefit of the flexibility and sensitivity of the rod, it must be held so that the direction of the pull is at right angles to the axis of the rod. If the fish is fairly close to the angler, this may mean holding the rod at an angle of forty-five degrees, not vertically. Now the tip and uppermost part of the rod are taking the strain with the minimum help from the butt. And this represents the most gentle use of the rod consistent with a reasonable degree of control. It is the way to use the rod towards the end of the fight, when the fish is rolling on the surface close at hand: gone is the water-cushion on the nylon which relieves the strain on the hook-hold, and this is now at its most vulnerable. (How many stories are there of fish of all sorts being lost at the very last moment?) If, at this stage, the rod is held at the vertical with the fish nearby, the tip takes the strain almost entirely on its own. It is a jerky business and there is a complete lack of control – the fish can swing round on the surface as if the rod were a maypole. And it will be appreciated that the longer the rod, the worse the situation if this particular mistake is made.

Actually the big carbon rods are strong enough to force the smallish salmon to the side long before they are played-out, by raising the rod smoothly until its axis is vertical and then, clearly one has no control over the fish. Obviously, of course, this is no fault of the rod in question and it would be just as much a mistake with any other rod, irrespective of the length or the material.

Next to be considered is the effect when the axis of the rod is lowered to angles of, say, sixty degrees down to thirty degrees, with the salmon some distance away so that the pull of the rod is considerably greater than ninety degrees. The lower the rod is held, the smaller is the share of the strain taken by the tip and the more the lower portions of the rod come into play. And with the rod at about thirty degrees, a tremendous amount of strain can be put on the salmon. This is what is meant by the old saying 'giving the fish the butt'. Naturally, it is a manoeuvre that is only used in fairly critical situations when the most drastic action is required in order to hold a salmon very firmly indeed, or to get it moving when it is lying doggo.

Let us now look at a few of the ways in which the angler uses his skill to make the most of the versatility of the action of the rod. Starting with the fish on a fairly short line and, therefore, the need to have the rod at an angle of, say, sixty degrees so that the pull of the line is at right angles to the axis, the salmon commences to make a run.

This should not be discouraged too forcefully, of course, because it is the effort of keeping on moving against controlled strain that tires the fish most. So the salmon fairly quickly increases the distance between itself and the rod. And it will be appreciated that as this takes place while the rod is kept at the angle of sixty degrees, the angle of pull of the line steadily increases, which is equal to a proportionate lowering of the rod. Thus the strain imposed on the fish by the rod gradually increases as the distance grows, which is just what is wanted.

Usually, when the angler performs in this way, a salmon does not run for more than about twenty-five to thirty yards. Then it tends to try and stay in the new position it has reached, but normally there is not much difficulty in recovering line steadily and bringing the salmon all the way back again. And if this sort of performance is repeated several times without any great complication, the salmon is soon subdued without any serious risk of losing it.

But, of course, few contests with salmon are quite as prosaic. And one must be ready to respond rapidly to any of the eventualities which may occur. One problem is when a fish leaps. If the hook-hold is at all vulnerable, this is accentuated while the fish is in the air. Also there is the risk that when it falls back onto the water, the salmon will drop on the leader and break it. Fortunately there is usually ample warning before a fish comes hurtling out of the water; it is preceded by a sudden big acceleration in the speed of the run and this gives just enough time to take whichever action is preferred. Some anglers believe in dropping the rod point in order to produce as much slack line as possible, and thus hopefully avoid undue strain on the hook-hold and the danger of the fish falling back onto a tight line.

Others have more confidence in raising the rod to the highest possible with the line free to run off against the check, but with the line otherwise kept tight. They consider this to be the best way of avoiding the worst risk – that of the fish falling back onto the leader. As far as the hook-hold is concerned, they take the view that if it is poor, it is going to part anyway, while if it is reasonably secure, it will stand up to the strain their method imposes.

Another complication that often arises, especially on the big rivers, is when the fish runs so far across the current that one has to raise the rod very high so that there is a minimum of line in or on the water. (Too much sunk line puts a tremendous amount of strain on the leader and hook-hold when a lively fish puts a spurt on.) It so happens, of course, that the angler is then in the position of causing the minimum resistance to the fish at a time when there is the great need to be increasing it in order to put an end to the run. However, while there is no disputing the dichotomy of this unavoidable situation, it will be appreciated how invaluable are the greater length of rod and the helpful characteristics of carbon. Indeed, if there is a prime argument for wanting a very long carbon rod, this is it.

At this stage the experienced angler looks for any advantage he may gain by any possible change of his position on the side of the river. It may be a good ploy to move downstream. This tends to reduce the pull of the current on any part of the line which may be sunk, and often it results in more of the line coming clear of the surface of the water. But it also tends to make the direction of the pull more downstream, and this can usually be expected to induce the salmon to change its course more towards the upstream direction, which helps in several ways. Firstly, it reduces the cross pull on the line from the current, and secondly it increases the amount of effort the fish has to make in order to maintain its movement. Usually the fish soon comes to a halt and from the new position on the bank it can be brought back more easily to a safer distance from the rod.

Eventually there are signs that the salmon is approaching exhaustion – a tendency to roll on its side and move round in small circles. Now all the strain required to bring the fish close to the edge of the water can be imposed with the axis of the rod at right-angles to the pull of the line, and as mentioned previously, this reduces any risk there may be of the hook tearing out. If the angler is alone and there is the possibility of beaching the fish, that is by far the safest procedure. The rod should be held horizontally – always with the line at right-angles, of course – as the fish is eased onto the pebbles. Care should be taken to ensure that the length of the leader plus some line, is about the same as the length of the rod so that once the salmon is lying on its side on the waterline the angler can point the rod inland as he moves round to the fish, then grasp it round the wrist of the tail and slide it head first up the pebbles. This is much safer than trying to lift the fish.

If it is not possible to beach a salmon, but help is available to tail, net or gaff it, the angler should again ensure that the line stays at right-angles. But in such a case, it is better to work with a few extra yards of line left out, and in order to maintain the maximum amount of control over the fish as it is brought to the edge, it is best to do this whenever possible by the angler stepping smoothly backwards rather than moving the rod only or reeling in more line.

The most difficult problem, of course, is when one is alone and there is no possibility of beaching the fish. (Incidentally, most experienced anglers would prefer to walk a fish up quite a long distance to beach it rather than to have to tail it, net it or gaff it single-handed.) Here again, the crucial factor at the final stage is to have the length of leader plus line exactly right. The rod will be at about forty-five degrees, the line at right-angles, and the fish feebly trying to keep on an even keel and to get further away. One chooses the right moment when the inclination of the fish is suitable to move the rod sideways and guide the fish head first towards the bank. Then smoothly the rod is raised to the vertical so that there is a continuous movement of the salmon right up to the hand, tailer, net or gaff. If the current near the side is rather heavy, it may be necessary for the angler to move downstream while he is raising the rod, but with tackle properly matched to the conditions one can have more confidence with the big carbon rod than anything that has been used in earlier days.

It will be appreciated that never, until this final moment when the exhausted fish is brought in to the unassisted angler, is the angle between the line and the rod allowed to be very much less than ninety degrees. This is the key to the efficient playing of a salmon and once one is familiar with the drill, there is not the slightest doubt that a long, properly designed carbon rod is found to be by far the best for playing a fish with fly tackle.

Chapter 17

The Sunk Line in Perspective

It is regrettable that some writers in the past have been too persuasive about sunk-line fishing with the big fly for salmon without giving sufficient attention to the question of selectivity regarding the class of water. Not surprisingly the effect has often been the reverse of what they had obviously hoped. Less experienced readers have enthusiastically expected success in water that was unfavourable. Their subsequent sense of failure has frequently been heightened by seeing fish caught on spinning tackle by other anglers. Then the inevitable has happened; they have switched their interest to bait fishing, found it more rewarding, and shelved their ideas of sunk-line fishing. And as their confidence in spinning has grown, the inducement to give the sunk line another trial has diminished, or perhaps entirely disappeared. In a great number of cases this is undoubtedly a great loss.

In order to establish soundly the very positive advantages that the sunk line can sometimes have over spinning, it is necessary to look at the question absolutely objectively, and not overstate its claims either in principle or practice. To start with, it must be acknowledged that spinning is a much more versatile and generally productive method, while the matter of the popularly declared preference for catching salmon on fly tackle must be put aside. Sunk-line fishing must be considered simply in the terms of its relative effectiveness as a method. And on that down to earth basis, it is quite definite that often it can prove so superior to spinning that few anglers can afford to ignore the sunk line.

Before going any further, it should be stipulated that sunk-line fishing with leads or weighted flies that are so heavy that casting is a messy, toilsome affair, must be excluded. This compromise certainly kills a lot of fish early in the season on waters with the fly only rule, but it is doubtful whether any of the anglers who practise it would do

85

so for choice. And none would deny that spinning would be easier, more pleasant, and more effective. Certainly nobody would attempt to interpret the catches that are made by fishing this way as being meritable for the sunk line method.

From that falsely-based extreme, let us go straight to the circumstances in which the sunk line and big fly method both have the advantage over spinning and gives the operational pleasure, so to speak.

When the water is very cold and the reactions of the fish are so slow that they need a long look at a big lure and the easiest possible chance to seize it, they favour a very gentle flow. With the large spinning bait, it is quite impossible always to fish as slowly as is desirable, the minimum speed that will hold the bait just clear of the bottom being too fast to allow it to hover for long within the comfortable taking range of the fish. Now, the combination of the time-tested oil-dressed silk line and the large fly dressed on any one of the popular types of unweighted irons, lends itself perfectly to the needs of the situation. No great skill is needed. After just a reasonable cast across and downstream, the balance of the tackle and the flow of the water is such that the fly comes round exactly as is wished.

In circumstances of this sort, sunk-line fishing can produce most wonderful sport and it is then without doubt the most efficient method.

Unfortunately the limitations concerning the depth and speed of the water are very narrow, and, of course, it is the failure of writers to stress this fact in many books that has led to so many anglers expecting too much of sunk-line fishing and being bitterly disappointed. Personal skill can, needless to say, widen the scope considerably, but as far as it concerns the average angler who cannot manage to get enough fishing hours to afford time for extended practice, it is best to accept as a fact that spinning will probably have the advantage, excepting at those times when water conditions are pretty well ideal for the sunk line.

The comparatively recently introduced fast-sinking lines have been thought by many anglers to offer the chance of a short cut to success with the sunk line method. Once again the very skilled angler can widen his scope by using the fast sinker when the river is higher and the water deeper and faster. But it cannot be stressed too strongly that it is useless to attempt to fish exclusively with the fast sinker. In the ideal conditions for sunk-line fishing as described earlier, the performance of the fast sinker is considerably less good even than that of spinning tackle. Any effort to make the fly fish very slowly – which is the objective – is ruined by the heavy line going straight to the bottom. As a second line, the fast sinker may be very useful. But where choice of method is allowed, it should be remembered that conditions that call for the fast sinker will usually mean that spinning will be the better way to ensure some sport.

At this juncture it may seem that the narrowing down of the circumstances that really favour sunk-line fishing puts it into a bracket of opportunities that are so rare that it is scarcely worth bothering with. That would be as wrong as making claims too sweeping for the method.

Most years bring long periods in the early part of the season when the suitable pools are at a more or less perfect level for sunk-line fishing. And there are quite a lot of rivers where the old style orthodox sunk-line fishing will account for a bigger aggregate catch than spinning if both methods are given their proper amount of attention in accordance with the state of the water day by day.

Finally there is a point in favour of sunk-line fishing that is perhaps not quite as peculiar as it seems at the first mention. Moving down the pool slowly and making a very thorough, close search with the sunk line does not disturb the fish and put them off nearly so much as spinning does. This proves to be so with such consistency that it must be deduced that the behaviour and appearance of spinners are much more potentially alarming to the fish than those of the large fly, despite the fact that the latter is accompanied by the considerably more visible line. However, this does mean that if there are restrictions regarding the amount of water available to the individual rod, the prospects of continuing to get response over a long period are better with the sunk line than with spinning. Similarly, if several anglers have to share the same stretch of water, they would be wise to refrain from spinning whenever conditions are reasonably good for sunk-line fishing.

Part Two

Sea-trout

Chapter 18

Thoughts on Sea-trout Fishing

There is a bigger variety of ways of catching sea-trout than any other fish. Each style has its devotees and it seems that sea-trout addicts have the fishing mania the most deeply rooted of all anglers. This is so, despite the fact that in any one particular area the sea-trout season is relatively of rather short duration. Much more of the year is spent in planning, preparing and dreaming than in actual fishing, yet this seems to increase the fervour rather than reduce it. So, it is not surprising that sea-trout fishers are extremely fussy about everything to do with their sport, including their ideas concerning what they require of their rods.

The most convenient way to make a run-down of the different methods is to start at the estuary, then work up through the sea pool and into the main river.

On the smaller rivers and spate streams, where one can cross the sands or pebbles at low tide and reach the channel that is then running strongly with fresh water, there is often the chance of the most hectic sport imaginable when the water is not coloured. Towards the end of the ebb and through the early stages of the making of the tide, while there is still a strong flow seawards, sea-trout of all sizes may be seen leaping. A 'terror' type of lure of about three inches long is frequently taken in a most violent fashion. And the sea-trout are inclined to fight like mad creatures – much more fiercely than anything you are likely to encounter in the actual river. Like most of the best things, though, the spell when sport can be had before the river starts to back-up is rather short, but it is long enough to make some splendid catches.

While that excitement is being enjoyed in the estuary, anglers in the sea pool and a little way upstream may be having their sport in many different ways – according to the height of the water and the state of the weather. With a good flow of water and particularly when it is

91

rather wet and windy, a team of three standard sea-trout patterns in medium sizes, say tens or eights, may prove successful on floating line, sink-tip, or, in a very fast current, on a slow sinker. At dusk and in the early part of the night, one would probably cut down to a single fly, or at the most two, of a larger size – six or even bigger – and probably favouring a pattern with plenty of black in it. All three types of line can still be effective, but many anglers would then put all their faith in sunk-line fishing.

In calmer weather in both these lower reaches of the river and higher upstream, there are sometimes opportunities to catch some fine sea-trout on dry fly. In the middle of the day a very small pale watery dun on a sixteen or at the largest a fourteen, is often the best pattern, while at dusk a medium sedge on a size twelve can be very effective. Many of the offers, especially when fishing fairly deep water, come in the form of beautiful head and tail rises. One just lets the fish get its head going down again and then tightens. On the fine nylon that is necessary, the sport that follows can be almost nerve-racking. Also at dusk and into the night, fishing with the wakefly can be most fascinating. A red sedge or a bushy black fly on a number eight and well greased – should be made to travel on the surface at about the same speed as the natural great red sedge cruises across the water to reach the bank or beach.

Often big sea-trout position themselves between the angler and the approaching artificial in order to head it off. Then the suspense waiting for the imminent attack is intense. Just a little tip here – keep your rod point very high at all times because when your wakefly is taken with a violent lunge away from you, a tight line almost certainly means a missed fish or a broken leader. The curve of the line to the water from the highly held rod tip gives the safety cushion of slack line both to let the sea-trout get its mouth properly closed before the setting of the hook and to ensure that the resultant pull on the rod tip, while the fish is still dangerously close, is at the angle which provides the maximum degree of flexibility.

In clearer water conditions on the middle and upper reaches of many rivers, including some of the very large ones, good sport is often to be had during good hatches of duns by fishing the wet fly in all respects as for brown trout. Particularly in the broken water where one would expect to do the best for brown trout, the so-called spider patterns of the North Country, such as Snipe & Purple, Snipe &

Yellow, Rough Bodied Poult, etc., – on sixteens and fourteens – may be taken very freely by the sea-trout. A notable feature of situations of this sort is that the sea-trout can become very selective when any one particular species of natural fly predominates. Even quite big specimens can show a pleasing readiness to rise to the emergent dun, but then, as with the brown trout, the pattern used has to be a very effective imitation if it is to deceive the sea-trout. With conditions much the same but in the absence of hatches, the standard sea-trout patterns in small sizes – fourteens and twelves – may have reasonable success. When the natural flies are around in good numbers, though, it certainly does pay to rely on the popular imitations of the species present.

In coloured water, particularly after the crest of the spate has passed downstream, the medium sizes of the standard patterns of sea-trout flies really come into their own. In those circumstances the novice often seems to think that it should pay to get the flies down to the fish with a sunk line. But two or three factors should be remembered. Sea-trout like to lie on the bottom when not on the move upstream, but also they like the clearer water in the surface areas better than the tainted stuff deep down. So, in order to lie on the bottom and still be near the surface, they have to pick the more shallow parts, often those very close to the side where so many anglers are tempted to wade and disturb the fish. Also, with the colour of the water reducing the range of vision of the fish, lures seen near the surface and against the lightest background make a much bigger impact than those appearing at the eye level of the fish and against the murky background along the horizontal plane.

Sea-trouting, of course, is by no means the monopoly of the river fishers. There are many very fine lochs which have a long and splendid reputation and which often produce an excellent average size of fish. Blow-line fishing is perhaps the most talked of style, but a great deal of fishing is done in the traditional way of making long drifts downwind in boats and using a team of three standard loch, lake or sea trout patterns, whichever you prefer to call them. Fishing a lure at a very fast speed by stripping line, dry fly fishing and even nymph fishing are also to be seen practised quite regularly these days. No doubt if one method fails, the enterprising modern angler is prepared to use his initiative to try something different and find a way of making a successful presentation.

The choice of rods is, of course, pretty obvious. On the stillwater, the light double-handed rod has quite a strong following and for those anglers the twelve foot *Grilse* is an ideal model. For fishing drifts with a single-handed rod and in the order of their lengths, the *Century Grilse* – eleven feet and three inches, the *Salmon and Sea Trout* – and the ten feet and six inches *Multi Trout* are all most suitable rods. For blow line the fifteen foot *Grilse* is the outstanding rod, but almost any of the double-handed salmon rods are plenty light enough for the work involved.

For estuary and river fishing the best all rounder is undoubtedly the *Salmon and Sea Trout*. It handles the sunk line perfectly, but is nevertheless very pleasant indeed to use with the floating line or sink-tip. The *Century Grilse* is a very fine rod for all floating-line fishing, but in view of the leverage of its eleven feet and three inches length, it is not recommended for the sunk line. The *Multi Trout* ten and ten feet six inch rods will both fish a light sunk line nicely, say a #five, but are much better for the floating line, their great charm for sea-trouting being when the more delicate forms of fishing – dry fly and brown trout patterns of wet fly – are the most promising.

The fight of an acrobatic sea-trout tends to make one forget everything but trying to do the right thing to ensure that it is successfully beached or brought to the net. But after gazing at your beautiful prize with satisfaction, you might reflect on how splendidly your fine carbon rod has served you?

Chapter 19

A River Run by Sea-trout and Salmon

When to fish and when to snatch sleep; when to try for salmon and when to concentrate on sea-trout; those are the questions in July.

The character of the river and the level of the water in the picture entitled 'our imaginary river' should satisfy our every wish. The problem, therefore, is almost entirely reduced to that of the overhead conditions. And the major decisions we must make will be based on our judgement of the trend of the weather.

The blue sky and light cloud promise pleasant warmth without it being oppressive. In sultry weather, we should be inclined to dismiss most of the hours of daylight as being unpromising. Then it would be easy to find time for rest so that the full pleasure could be got from a whole night's sea-trouting. But in the prevailing circumstances, full consideration must be given both to daytime fishing and to operations during the night.

Fortunately there are a few very reliable general guides to help us. The observance of these should ensure that any mistakes we make will not be very serious. And our faith in these guides will be equally great, whether or not we are familiar with the particular river or the area in which it lies.

First and foremost we know that in the current circumstances we should never neglect to fish during the late evening and the early part of the night. And those among us with the necessary will power will ensure that they are always at the riverside to greet the dawn, when salmon are often easier to catch than at any other time. Next, during the later morning there are grounds for hoping that the salmon will show some interest. The most meaningful indication of their being in a responsive mood would be to see some head-and-tail rises. In that case, if we fail to secure some sport we should have to concede the fault to be our own. Towards noon there will be good prospects of a hatch of pale watery duns to attract the sea-trout and offer the chance of a spell of fascinating dry fly fishing.

During the early afternoon, little will be lost if we take the opportunity to get some rest. If a good breeze were to get up we should not rule out the possibility of raising a salmon, but otherwise it is the best policy to leave the fish in peace during this, the hottest part of the day.

The period between about five o'clock and eight o'clock is unlikely to be very promising, but there is always the possibility of the salmon or sea-trout becoming interested. In such a case, however, there is sure to be some visible activity to reveal it. And unless such evidence is forthcoming, it is still best to leave the water undisturbed.

After that, we should certainly be on the spot to watch the reaction of the fish during the approach to sunset and dusk.

In the light of these factors, the general plan we decide upon is that the time we can most safely allow for sleep is between lunch and dinner. Then we must eat well so that we shall not have to worry about food again for many hours.

Before settling the details of our fishing tactics, we must make an evaluation of the characteristics of the water and of any special or unusual features that are probable. We note first that it is a semi-gorge type of stretch (it bears the signs of being fed by a large sheet of still water, not very far away), with a series of relatively short, distinctly separate pools. There is literally no barren water and the pools are capable of holding a very heavy stock of both salmon and sea-trout. Deep water for daytime retreat and splendid runs and glides are plentiful. The aeration should be adequate to ensure good spells of sport both by day and at night, excepting in the worst of hot, close weather. In addition to all those desirable features, we should also recognise that this class of water lends itself to the inclusion of two specially valuable types of summertime salmon lies that often yield well in the daytime when fish in other positions are completely disinterested. The kind likely to be the most numerous is that found where a large boulder or outcrop of rock in deepish, medium-paced water, causes a stronger flow towards the surface. Fish usually lie above and slightly ahead of such obstructions, and their presence there is a certain indication of their being at least in a favourably disposed mood. Much less common – perhaps the rarest sort of lie – is a mid-water position in a glide where the pull from two separate heads of a run cause an invisible parting of the flow. The foreground of the picture shows a possibly perfect example of such a lie. The glide divides at its extremity into two distinct flows, and that will almost certainly create a point in the apparently even flow of the glide where a fish can enjoy the benefit of very fast water without any effort to maintain its position. Salmon that rest in such places – often running fish – are almost certain takers.

Lastly, but not the least important, we note the proximity of shade-giving and food-harbouring trees. A plentiful supply of insect life to keep the sea-trout on the *qui vive* is ensured, while, as time goes along, we feel sure that we shall be able to exploit the advantages of the shadows from the trees, especially during the evenings.

Our fishing on the first day will presumably start after breakfast. We will begin in the run near the head of the pool, like the rod in the picture. In view of the light and bearing in mind the presence of grilse and sea-trout as well as salmon, we put on a small Silver Blue – a number ten should be about right. If we hook a salmon in the run, which is the easiest to fish correctly, we shall concentrate on similar places in each pool, and will have no time to spare for the other types of flow. But should the run be unproductive, we would give the glide a trial, and fish it right up to the lip to the rapid. There in the glide a heavier and rather bigger fly is necessary, preferably a black-bodied pattern to make a more definite impact in the fast water. A heavy-ironed double number eight Blue Charm should behave correctly. And if we find a successful cast there, we shall mark it carefully for future reference.

As lunchtime approaches, the pale watery duns and some small light sedges become numerous. We see a dimple as one disappears, and we keep watch. Soon it happens again and we realise that it was quite a good sea-trout that rose from the depths and took the insect with hardly any disturbance of the surface. Now our dry fly sails over the same place, and we strike instantly we see it touched. Then the pool explodes and eventually we are as proud of our two and a half pound sea-trout on a very fine cast as any fish we have ever caught.

A drink and a chat over lunch is followed by a shower and bed. We think we shall not sleep, but the air and the contentment of mind work miracles. When the call comes half an hour before the dinner gong, we cannot believe we have been asleep longer than a few minutes, but we shall feel the benefit in the early hours of the morning.

Back at the river again with the shadows lengthening, we first try for salmon on similar lines to our morning efforts. We see a fish perform a couple of head-and-tail rises half-way down the pool in the shade of the big tree. That tells us all we want to know. On goes a number seven Blue Charm, and the delightful take comes at the second cast. We let him go well down again with the fly – really only a matter of a second or so – before we tighten very gently. Then the grilse gives a running battle such as no other fish can emulate.

We take the tip to concentrate on shaded water until sunset. Now we have a difficult but pleasant choice to make. Shall we fish a dry sedge for sea-trout, or a number six Blue Charm and hope for a salmon, or perhaps a big sea-trout? The now noisy activity of the sea-trout decides the matter for us, and we lay aside the salmon rod.

A number three Medium Sedge, well greased, and sometimes dragging a little, gets plenty of attention from the fish, and as with the dry artificial pale watery, we strike instantly. As the light begins to go, we change to a number five bushy Black Zulu, but still well greased. This we keep moving across the surface at about the speed of a natural Great Red Sedge. When the sea-trout comes, it is a vicious attack, and although we strike instantly, we think that perhaps he had already hooked himself.

We realise that this sort of sport could perhaps continue, with odd quietish intervals, throughout the night, but we wish also to try the glides at the tails of the pools with sunk sea-trout patterns. Meantime, however, there have been some furrows revealing restlessness among the salmon, we put on a double number eight Black Doctor, and where the current slackens, we help the fly along by coiling some line. When the pull is felt we strike, but have no means of knowing at that moment whether it is a salmon, a grilse or a big sea-trout.

We feel, too, that this method would keep us happily occupied for most of the hours of darkness, but already we have a nice mixed basket, and knowing there are some specimen sea-trout about, we decide to try for one in the tail of the pool. The end of the line is degreased with a solution of Fuller's Earth, and a strong, two-fly cast is mounted. At the point is a number eight Silver March Brown – some people would prefer a big streamer fly – and the dropper is a number six Grouse and Claret.

98

Now we must be alive to something very different in the way of the behaviour of the sea-trout. A little fish will perhaps give a heave as heavy as those that come when the fly is fished nearer the surface. But with the well-sunk artificial, the take of a big fish can be the gentlest of draws. We therefore tighten at the slightest indication that the fly is not travelling freely. Sometimes the cast will have just touched a stone, but sooner or later it could be the real thing, and then we should be ready for anything to happen. A big sea-trout can be very lazy and dour, but equally he can go berserk, and as likely as not he will have a lot of backing out several times before he is subdued.

A good night with the sea-trout passes very quickly and sooner than expected comes the false dawn. Then is the time to get ready for an attempt for any specially big salmon that is known to be in any particular lie. As the light begins to grow from the east, fish, like most animals, seem to have their careless moment. But by the time one salmon has been landed, the best of the opportunity is over; hence the careful use of it for selected fish only. A good-sized – say number five – dark fly is advisable, and it is usually best to fish it as slowly as possible.

Before the sun appears on the horizon, the fish assume their normal daytime caution. The early morning should, of course, still provide opportunities of sport with skilful fishing. Indeed, many anglers consider this to be by far the best part of the day. Certainly it should be used to the best advantage lest a change in the weather puts the fish into a poor mood for all further daytime fishing.

Chapter 20

By Night for Sea-trout?

'Never disturb the pool until the last light of day has gone!' That is often repeated, and by so many sea-trout fishers is believed to be sound policy that to disobey it feels almost to be poaching. Yet the failing light and dusk often offer the best and sometimes only opportunity of sport with these exciting fish.

The approach to the problem requiring that the angler should be denied this delightful spell is perhaps not very penal as far as seasoned night fishers are concerned. It is not every angler, however, who can settle down happily to fish in the dark. Considerable numbers abandon all efforts to get used to night fishing because they regretfully discover that they simply cannot concentrate when they are not able to see in detail what they are doing. For them, discouragement about fishing around dusk is obviously to be deplored and therefore, for their sake and that of novices, a re-examination of the habits of sea-trout, with emphasis on that particular question, is much overdue.

Without any risk of robbing the sea-trout of his somewhat mystic charm, it can be said that his life as an adult fish in fresh water is not at all difficult to understand – he is, in fact, an uncomplicated fish. He has a big appetite, is an aggressive feeder, and is extremely fond of flies. It so happens, though, that in the normally warm weather of the period when the sea-trout begin to arrive in big numbers, there is not much regular, worthwhile fly life on the water during the daytime, then the fish rest in the security of the deep pools, preferably under trees. Apart from being tempted by the occasional dun, spinner, or titbit that drops from the leaves, they lie quietly waiting for the great feast that they can expect when the light begins to fade.

It is well to remember here that any good sea-trout river when fully stocked has to carry a far greater head of fish than could be supported

100

if they were brown trout and had to be accommodated throughout the year. Consequently the fish are usually found to be in dense concentrations in the more desirable places. And whether or not they have the instinct to shoal, they have no choice than to behave as if that were their inclination.

Even from late evening onwards, when sea-trout are well distributed over all the best feeding areas, they are necessarily comparatively close together. Consequently, they get the benefit of the shoal system of warning. But the alarms are not remembered indefinitely as some would have us believe. When the feast starts, often well in advance of the night proper, the distress of a hooked fish causes a minimum of upset amongst the others and sea-trout frequently are brought to the net in quick succession.

Admittedly when the expected fare is not forthcoming, a serious disturbance will make them vacate their prospective feeding stations. But this applies during the night as well as at dusk, and in any case – even when there is no reason for the sea-trout to be scared – they do not remain indefinitely in any one place if their search for food there is unsuccessful. Furthermore, whatever the cause of their departure, they return rapidly to the advantageous positions where there are flies to be had.

Nevertheless, it must be recognised that anglers who solemnly adhere to the principle that operations should never commence until nightfall, presumably consider that the controlling characteristic of the sea-trout is extreme shyness – especially in the day-time – and that once their suspicions have been aroused it takes a long time for them to settle down again into a responsive mood. These people seem to get the idea chiefly from the fact that certain methods employing large, slow-moving lures are not – in a clear water – effective until dark, but that cannot be accepted as the proof of shyness that it is assumed to be. It is far more likely that the failure of the big artificials before dark is because the fish do not associate them with the then ruling conditions and do not see natural creatures of similar size and behaviour until night-time. That explanation would seem to be confirmed by the frequent ready response of the sea-trout towards dusk to smaller artificials more in keeping with natural flies which they expect to see at that time, even though the latter are not currently in evidence. Furthermore, reasonably cautious fishing with suitable flies before the arrival of darkness does not put the fish down, either immediately or subsequently, and most anglers are well able to demonstrate that if they try.

Thus the interpretation of the ordinary available evidence can only reasonably be that the food situation is the decidedly dominant influence in the habits of the sea-trout, and not an undue tendency to shyness. Strategy can therefore safely be based on the simple fact that if the fly food is available, the sea-trout will be in the best feeding positions and ready to respond providing that just ordinary precautions are observed. If there are no flies excepting around dusk – no amount of skill makes very much difference and the catches will not be heavy.

It is chiefly a matter, then, of trying to judge if and when there will be a suitable number of flies. Everybody is familiar with the warm, humid conditions that are the most favourable and in that respect there are no difficulties. Unfortunately, however, the change from day to night is subject to being accompanied by a very marked and sudden change in the state of the atmosphere. Frequently a late evening that looks most promising is followed by a rapidly clearing sky and quick drop in temperature. Conversely, very indifferent weather before dark can develop into more or less what is wanted when the night begins.

The common belief that most creatures of nature are instinctively aware of coming changes in the weather does not seem to hold good in the respect of the sea-trout's ability correctly to foresee the non-arrival of the much wanted flies. Almost without fail and regardless of the weather, they are alerted by the change of light as dusk approaches. Then, as previously indicated, all the good casts will usually yield fish for at least a short spell, irrespective of the presence or otherwise of natural flies.

If the flies do not materialise, the river eventually goes dead and fishing is pretty useless, but that applies whether or not the feeding fish have been covered by the angler during dusk. When a plentiful supply of flies does appear, the brisk sport of dusk continues well into the night with, perhaps occasional gaps that coincide with the spells when for some reason or other the flies become temporarily scarce.

Should all activity stop with the arrival of darkness however, the angler who has started soon enough might well already be generously rewarded for his visit to the river. And such a sea-trout fisher will no longer heed the warnings that the shyness of the fish dictates the sacrifice of that invaluable period of sport around dusk.

The newcomer to sea-trout will probably find it very difficult to avoid involvement in the acute partisanship which persists on most rivers concerning the method of presenting the fly. If his own preferences and judgement are to have much chance, he must first appreciate one extraordinary aspect of the sport.

It is this: the really dashing, furious fighting ability of the sea-trout, that has had such a thrilling appeal to all generations of fly-fishers, is much more a feature of the medium-sized and smaller ones than of the big specimens.

The latter, nevertheless, tend to steal all the glamour. But they – upwards of six pounds – are usually relatively very old fish and they both behave and taste like it too! Their comparatively sluggish, bottom-hugging opposition to the rod is such, nevertheless, that if it happens to be the angler's first introduction to the sport with sea-trout – either personally or as a witness – he will probably think it practically impossible for anything to be better. Then he is in danger of concentrating too much on the deeply-sunk, large flies that are favoured by the big-specimen addicts.

If the angler with all-round experience deliberately chooses that method, there is no need for comment. The desire of everyone to have some big sea-trout in his personal record must be sympathetically acknowledged. But the newcomer should certainly at least give a trial to fishing near and on the surface with the smaller flies before deciding to settle down permanently to the single-minded quest to beat his previous best fish.

A good night with the big sea-trout undoubtedly does much for the ego; that is not thought by all, though, to be enough compensation for the loss of hectic sport available with the smaller fish. Indeed, the way in which two or three-pounders often strip off all the line and a lot of backing in an amazing display of speed and strength – punctuated by fantastic leaps – is considered by many widely experienced anglers, including some big-game fishers, to be the finest sport that is to be had with any fish in the world.

Additionally it is well to remember that the big fish can be very moody and dour, even when everything seems to be favourable. Against that, the smaller sea-trout can be relied upon to respond readily whenever the circumstances give them the slightest encouragement. The big fish may be dominant in the record book, but in the memory it is more often the smaller fish that are supreme!

Another consideration which should also be recognised is that there are usually worthwhile numbers of grilse and small summer salmon around when sea-trout fishing is in full swing. The larger fly near the bottom is most unlikely ever to interest these other fish, but it is not at all uncommon at both sides of dusk for them to take the popular standard sea-trout patterns close to the surface.

For a good mixed bag, however, small salmon flies provide the best all-round prospects. In the late evening, when the fish leave the deeper water in favour of the fast run towards the head of a pool, a Blue Charm on a number six low water iron takes a lot of beating; even a good brown trout will then have a go at it too. In the smoother glides, or where the current becomes steadier and it is necessary to coil some line to help the fly to fish properly, the low water iron will probably be too light. The patent type of 'short-point double' – say a number eight – is ideal and a Black Doctor is a very suitable dressing. What is more, the big sea-trout do not ignore these small salmon flies. But it is not at all uncommon to be recorded – quite innocently – as salmon, and they might well be quite a lot bigger than the grilse and small summer fish that are taken.

Dry-fly fishing though, has some inherent valuable advantages when sea-trout are the sole objective. For most anglers the visual interest is an extra fascinating feature. This is perhaps at its greatest premium before dark, when a medium sedge is justifiably the most popular fly. But even on quite dark nights it is surprising how the disturbance on the surface, when the fish takes, causes either a break or an increase in the reflection, which can easily be detected. And even when nothing can be seen at all, the exciting smack of the take can be heard, and gives warning to strike. In such conditions a well greased Black Zulu seems to be more attractive than the bustard type patterns. If it is fished right into the side at about the speed of the natural Great Red Sedge, the sea-trout will often swirl within a foot or two of the angler as they turn rapidly in their manoeuvres to head-off the fly, and then take it just before it would, otherwise, be lifted from the water.

From the physical point of view, the dry fly is easier to control effectively, and is much more trouble-free than a team of wet flies. But perhaps the most important thing about the floating artificial –

which is shared to a lesser degree by the heavy fly fished just beneath the surface – is that it can be worked with very good prospects of success over slack areas that often hold a lot of fish, and which are practically useless for the more practised methods.

In most fly-fishing for species other than sea-trout, it is usually an obvious matter to decide which will probably be the best way to take full advantage of the particular circumstances. Failing that, there will be little doubt as to the two alternatives that might have equally good claims for a trial, and one of which will probably be the correct answer. The position in regard to sea-trout can be much the same as far as the individual is concerned, but it is unlikely that there will ever be agreement among several anglers. The interesting controversy starts up again, and if the prejudices can be subdued sufficiently, the exchange of ideas can often be most profitable.

All methods of fishing are undoubtedly the development of what started out originally as individual styles. In sea-trout fishing this process is still very much alive today and there are good chances for any angler to make exciting new discoveries if he refuses to be hidebound by old, unimaginative ideas.

Chapter 21

A Memorable Fish

On a lovely day in May a few years ago I was introducing John Winter, Secretary of the Bishop Auckland Club, to a beat on the middle reaches of the Lune. The water was in fine order, with a sprinkling of salmon and good sea-trout around.

A trickle hatch of medium olives got the wild brown trout moving nicely. I was tempted to put up a light trout rod with a DT4F line and a size sixteen dry John Storey on a two-pound point, and began in the tail of the pool well clear of John's operations.

After a short spell of excellent sport with the hard-fighting brownies I saw a rise to a dun which gave the distinct impression of a very big specimen on the feed. It was a fairly long cast but the fly dropped suitably and after drifting little more than a foot it was taken with a deliberate, seemingly slow but classic head-and-tail rise. I tightened and instantly the water exploded as a great bar of silver flung itself into the air. My little reel shrieked as the first run took out all the line and a lot of backing.

John saw what was happening and came running down. I confessed that I had no real hope of subduing such a fish on the tackle I was using, but I was going to try my best. After each of a succession of long runs, I managed to recover a lot of line and eventually there was some semblance of a slight degree of control being established. Indeed John got ready with the net in the very shallow water beside the smooth, almost flat, shingle beach where I was standing.

Time after time I got the fish coming towards the net, but then it saw John and set off again at a tremendous pace. Half an hour had now gone by and I said that the only desperate hope was for me to go well back from the water's edge and try to beach the fish with John standing well clear but ready to dash up and grab the fish if I could get it on its side.

It worked. Triumphantly John lifted up a beautiful, fresh-run sea-trout of four and a half pounds.

Part Three

Trout

Chapter 22

Introduction

All the game fish of the British Isles are members of the salmon family and they can be identified as such by the presence of the adipose fin, a small, fleshy, rounded appendage situated between the dorsal fin and the tail. They comprise the Atlantic salmon, the trout (both the migratory and non-migratory varieties), the grayling and an immigrant species from North America, the rainbow trout. All are bred in fine shingle in highly oxygenated water, which must be almost entirely free from pollution. No doubt this contributes to the fact that game fish make excellent eating, but of even greater importance to the angler are the influences of these environmental requirements of the fish on the methods of angling for them and the quality of sport they provide.

The key factor is the type of food upon which they live from the time when the young fish must fend for themselves. This is almost certain to include – or indeed, to consist entirely of – some type of aquatic fly life, probably in the form of larvae or nymphs.

The protein value of this food is very high and promotes great strength. The result is that fly-fishing is the basic method for all species and the hooked fish give splendid accounts of themselves before they can be subdued. There are also styles of bait fishing, more particularly those employing artificial lures, that are deemed to meet the sporting standards required in game fishing. Nevertheless, these are largely regarded as complementary methods to be resorted to only when circumstances are not favourable for fly-fishing.

Our first thoughts of fly-fishing may be restricted to sunny days in spring, but in fact there is not a single day in the year when, weather and water conditions permitting, it is not possible to have some exciting sport with the fly tackle and, on many occasions during all the seasons of the year, one is spoilt for choice – it is difficult to decide

111

which of several promising and fascinating options should be followed. This, of course, calls for some versatility but, given that, there is no closed season for the fly fisher.

The natural progression for the angler taking up fly fishing is to concentrate almost entirely on one style – probably dictated by the type of fishing most readily available to him – until he is reasonably proficient, and then to try his hand at other methods. This is very sound but at the same time there are great advantages to be gained in the way of appreciating more fully the principles governing the chosen method, if these can be considered alongside those applicable to the other methods. Practical points to be mentioned later will show the truth of this better than abstract discussion, so for the present let us agree that the first vital step is to get a concise overall picture of all the basic styles of fishing.

Because the dry fly is fished on the surface and everything, including the mistakes made by the angler, can be observed relatively easily and clearly, this method provides the most simple introduction to the subject, although that does not mean that it is the easiest one in which to gain a good degree of proficiency. Indeed, the skills of the successful dry-fly fisher include a sound knowledge of the habits of the fish, the water-bred flies upon which they feed, of the nature of river flows, of the various procedures collectively known as river craft, and the ability to cast and present the artificial fly with delicacy and accuracy. Armed with those capabilities it is only really a question of a small degree of adjustment for the individual to master any other form of fly-fishing.

Chapter 23

Dry-fly Fishing

In the classic scenario of dry-fly fishing the plump brown trout of the chalk or limestone-stream is seen to be 'on the fin'. This is the term used when the fish is fully alert and not lying dormant – the difference between the two postures is unmistakable. If the duns or spinners are drifting down and over the fish in quick succession, it will probably be stationed only a few inches beneath the surface so that it can put up its snout and intercept the food with the greatest efficiency. In such a position, close to the surface, its field of view of the approach of the flies is rather narrow but that is of no disadvantage when they are sufficiently plentiful to keep the fish busy without having to move very far sideways. When there are fewer flies, however, the feeding fish tends to lie a little deeper, thus giving itself visual command of a greater surface area ahead.

The problem could hardly be more simple in principle, but it is not always so simple in its practical solution. All the angler has to do is cast a suitably deceptive artificial to a point a foot or so ahead of the lie and let it drift down over the fish in exactly the same manner as the naturals. This must be achieved without disturbing the fish, which usually means that it must be completely unaware of the presence of the angler.

When the fish takes the artificial, the angler allows sufficient time for it to close its mouth properly (of which more later) and then tightens smoothly and firmly to set the hook. Now the line must be kept tight onto the fish at all times, with the angle of pull as high as possible. Thus with the rod held near the vertical, the fish feels more or less the same degree of restraint in whichever direction it attempts to move, including downwards, and can be played and guided away from weeds and other obstacles until it is finally brought over the net and lifted from the water.

113

The first difficulty, having spotted the interested trout, is to get into a suitable casting position without putting the fish down, or scaring it away altogether. The most important thing is to keep off the sky-line and it may be necessary to creep and crawl to do this. There must be no quick or jerky movement, nor any heavy footsteps. The lateral line of the fish is highly sensitive to vibrations in the water and the dropping of the net onto the bank would be certain to set the trout scuttling away. Having the sun behind you must also be avoided so that the shadow from the rod when casting will not fall across the lie. According to the location of weed beds and, perhaps, the branches of a tree in relation to the lie of the fish, the casting position selected will usually be in the area between a point more or less opposite to the fish and another as far downstream as will be permitted by the length of line that can be fished.

What is probably the most critical factor in dry-fly fishing now comes into play. The artificial must be placed on the water and made to drift over the trout without any unnatural movement caused by the leader or line restraining the free travel with the flow.

Any such check to the progress of the artificial is called drag and, even if it appears to be only very slight, it is almost certain to put the fish off. The tendency towards drag and the means of overcoming it vary a great deal in the different types of flow and, other factors permitting – such as the location of weed beds, branches of trees, etc. – this has to be taken into consideration when deciding which is likely to be the best position from which to cast.

The appearance of the surface of the water is very deceptive in respect of the extent to which it will cause drag. The extremely smooth surface of a fast, even-paced glide will probably look as if it will be easy to deal with but it is, in fact, the most difficult. If the line thrown is straight, the only angle which it is at all possible to avoid drag is in direct line with the flow and even then there is a big risk that the artificial will be pulled downstream at a faster rate than the flow, which is drag. (The reason is that the pace of the glide is likely to be faster at its lower extremity than it will be higher up.)

However, if the cast is made at a fairly narrow angle upstream and a lot of little wiggles are put into the line as it alights on the water, the fly will usually drift without any objectionable drag (while the curls in the line are straightening out) for the vital foot or so as it covers the fish.

Again, contrary to appearance, the type of water that presents the least problem concerning drag is the popply-looking stream. Providing the line or leader does not traverse a band of flow which is faster than that where the fly is required to be placed, a straight line will usually be satisfactory, and this may be so with a fairly square cast. The result is that in this class of water the angler has a much wider range of choice in the position he can select for casting. In view of the other variable factors such as the direction of the light, bank obstructions and the rest, the help this greater freedom can give may be quite invaluable.

Without any further delay it must be mentioned that when the cast is made at a narrow angle upstream and the flow is fairly fast, line must be retrieved in the free hand at a suitable rate to ensure that, when the rod is raised to hook the trout, there will be no undue amount of slack line to cause delay. With the squarish cast very little slack line is created while the fly is drifting over the lie – which can be an important consideration, especially when it is necessary to throw a long line in the first place simply to reach the fish.

Practice, of course, is essential in dealing with drag. Careful attention to the principles involved can save the almost endless frustration which becomes inevitable if too casual a view is taken of the importance of the different types of flow. Indeed, this question of drag remains permanently the great test of the dry-fly fisher and it is as if the trout recognise this fact, because the best fish always seems to occupy the lie where the drag problem is the greatest. Of course, it is easy to see why this is so. The check on the movement of the water caused by weeds and bank protrusions results in an acceleration in the flow adjacent, unobstructed area, and it is in speedier spots of this sort that the food drifts over the fish more quickly and hence in greater quantity. The fast water itself is not the difficulty with regard to drag. It is the fact that the line or leader is restrained by the steadier water close by. The feature of drag which ensures that it must always be considered apprehensively is that the permissible scope for trial and error is extremely small. Each time the artificial passes close to the trout incorrectly – that is, with easily visible drag – the less chance there is that the fish will be deceived when eventually an apparently suitable presentation is achieved.

No two lies are exactly alike and the flow at any one of them requires separate and detailed examination. Familiarity with the beat should, however, lead to the ability to deal quite satisfactorily with the majority of situations on the day. The inevitable failures here and there serve to make one suitably pleased with the better part of one's performance without any risk of becoming complacent about the problems of drag.

Coupled with the question of how the floating artificial behaves during the vital final approach to the feeding trout, there is always the complex problem of how it is seen by the eye of the fish, to what extent it succeeds in simulating the natural food and, indeed, whether or not effective imitation is important.

It must be said straight away that the way in which anglers cope with the subject in practice varies enormously. Some who enjoy a well above average amount of success get along with the minimum of knowledge of both entomology and the available artificials. They rely on a few favourite dressings and tend to assert that the standard of presentation is much more important than the actual pattern used.

There will be more on this point later, but for the moment let us say that such people use skills (almost amounting to a sixth sense) which are quite beyond the capability of the newcomer to the sport. The only safe course for the novice is to make a small study, which most will find enjoyable, of the life-cycles of the main kinds of flies and the details of the particular species most important in the diet of the fish. Then, as practical experience grows, the novice angler will become comfortably familiar with the naturals and their imitations and will make his selection of the pattern to be used with ever-growing and gratifying self-confidence.

By far the most important naturals so far as the dry-fly fisher is concerned are the upright-winged flies, including the famous mayfly, which belong to the family Ephemeridae. A nymph hatches from an egg at the bottom of the river and this small creature usually lives in the water for about a year, but in the case of the mayfly it will probably be two years. When the growth of the nymph has ceased and it stops feeding, it soon rises to the surface and the winged fly emerges from the nymphal case or, as the angler says, the dun hatches. After spells varying from a few minutes to a day or more according to the species, the dun undergoes a further metamorphosis and the fully mature fly, the spinner, emerges.

It is at this stage that mating takes place. This is the final act of the male but the female still has to deposit the eggs on or in the water.

116

Soon afterwards there is what is called a 'spinner fall'. The dead spinners drift down the river and are obviously thoroughly enjoyed by the trout.

The species of duns which the trout seem to like best and which appear commonly enough and in sufficiently large numbers to be of serious interest to the angler are relatively few.

The principal ones are the large spring olive or large dark olive, which appears early in the season – March/April; the March brown and the false or late March brown – March, April and early May; the medium olive – April and then on and off for the rest of the season; the iron blue – late April, May, and perhaps early June; the mayfly or green drake – late May/early June; the blue winged olive – June until the end of the season; and the pale watery – June onwards.

The times of appearance of the different species can vary considerably as a result of unseasonable weather and, of course, there are variations according to the character of the water and the general area of the surrounding country.

Some of the spinners have famous names. The March brown spinner is the Great Red Spinner. The male iron blue spinner is the Jenny Spinner. The medium olive spinner is the Red Spinner and the blue winged olive spinner is the Sherry Spinner.

No mention has yet been made of the beauty of the duns and spinners. In colouring, shape and movement most species are exceedingly attractive and this adds a great deal of charm and also interest to the study of the flies.

The other interesting families are the Trichoptera, the caddis or sedge flies; the Perlidae, the stone flies; and the Diptera, the gnats, crane flies, ants and beetles. In all these cases the fly that emerges from the larva is the final, mature form of the species, there being no further change. The floating representations of some of these flies are very popular on a local basis in certain circumstances – for example, a dry sedge at dusk in summer – but, in the main, they are of more interest to the wet-fly fisher.

It is also necessary to become familiar with some of the dressings with very well known names which do not necessarily indicate the species of flies which their inventors intended them to represent. Greenwell's Glory and the Gold Ribbed Hare's Ear are both commonly used and mainly in the belief that they are taken for the medium olive dun. The Little Marryat was designed to imitate the

117

pale watery dun. Then there are such highly popular patterns as the Grey Duster, the John Storey and the Sturdy's Fancy, each of which may represent more than one species reasonably well.

From this it will be clear that the dry-fly fisher must have a personal plan or scheme to ensure that he always has an adequate stock of flies at hand. At the same time this should not be too large for convenient use and, of course, not too expensive to acquire. Equally clearly this cannot be done on a rule of thumb basis without years of experience to produce the guidelines. If there is, indeed, a true short-cut to success in mastering this question of dry fly patterns, it is to read some of the popular books on anglers' entomology. However, this can be quite rewarding in its own right apart from the practical usefulness to be gained and it should not prove a chore to anyone who is naturally attracted to fly-fishing.

A good understanding of the required behaviour of the floating artificial – drifting without drag and riding high on the hackle points to simulate the posture of the natural dun – is the best guide to the type of tackle that is most suitable. Obviously the point of the leader must be fine enough for it not to be seen too easily by the fish and it must be sufficiently supple because stiffness may contribute towards drag. In practice it is found that nylon of about three pounds test is the best all round compromise. If one hooks a very heavy fish near dense growths of weed, one is inclined to wish that this weakest link in the chain were a good bit stronger, but at the same time one recognizes that the offer from the fish would probably not have come had the nylon not been so fine. The compromise that has to be made between fineness and strength can often be a key factor and is common to all styles of fly-fishing.

Knotless tapered leaders are available in all the various strengths that may be required. From three pounds test at the point ranging up to about ten pounds at the loop is probably the most popular for trouting with small flies. Some anglers make up their leaders with short strands of different strengths joined by blood knots.

A regular steep taper will be found suitable in most situations, but there is a popular belief that a better turnover of the leader can be achieved by using a double taper – that is, having thicker nylon in the middle than at the loop. This is a subject the individual may find worth investigating.

Leaders with fine points require light fly lines to match them

118

because the weight of the line imposes much strain that has to be borne by the leader at such crucial moments as when a fish is being hooked, or if it makes a violent jerk during the ensuing fight. Unfortunately, however, the novice usually finds that it is much easier to cast with a line that is rather heavier than the size that makes the safest partner for the leader. And this position is further aggravated by the fact that the heavier the line, the more difficult it is to present the fly with delicacy and a minimum of disturbance. Consequently, if the effort is made in the first place to master the casting with a suitably fine fly line, a lot of other potential difficulties for the future are made much easier to deal with. In this context it should be mentioned that, weight for weight, the traditional oil-dressed silk line is easier to cast with than the plastic-coated floater because its smaller bulk causes less air resistance. But the silk line requires constant care and attention – drying, cleaning, greasing, etc. – to ensure that it does not fail to float well enough during spells of sustained fishing, whereas the plastic line should give a reliably satisfactory performance at all times without the need for treatment any more complicated than keeping it free from surplus water and dirt.

The range of sizes in both silk and plastic lines is both wide and detailed enough to suit every need. And when eventually the selection has been made there will be plenty of scope for a choice of rods to balance the line. But first one should consider the other duties – besides straight-out dry-fly fishing for river trout – for which the outfit will probably be wanted. If the secondary role is to be river fishing with wet fly and nymph, the emphasis should be in favour of the finest line that can be managed suitably well – a number one or two silk or an AFTM four or five floater. On the other hand if some dry-fly work on stillwater or some sea-trouting is to have a fairly high priority, it would probably be best to go for a number three or four silk or an AFTM six or seven floater.

Probably the most popular length for a dry-fly rod at present is eight feet six inches, but this is largely a hangover from the days before the appearance of modern glass rods when there were good practical reasons for keeping the rod down to this length. Today, well designed glass rods are so light in weight and so versatile in the line sizes they will carry that these factors need no longer be at all restrictive in considering the length of rod to be chosen. Generally speaking – and ignoring the question of possible personal preference – there is no reason why a dry-fly rod should be as short as eight feet and six inches or less, except on water where casting space is badly restricted by thick foliage. Wherever there is enough space to use a long rod it is almost invariably an advantage. Nine feet is probably as long as most anglers would care to see a dry-fly rod, but this extra six inches makes a remarkable difference in several important respects, including the casting range, ground clearance on the back cast, taking up any unavoidable slack when striking and in the handling of a hard-fighting fish. The extra six inches can also be very helpful in all the secondary roles of the outfit, whether it is for the more delicate work with nymphs and wet flies or the sturdier duties with the sea-trout and on stillwater.

Sometimes it is said that the reel of the fly fisher is not important – nothing more than a receptacle to hold the line. The fallacy of this view cannot be appreciated to the full until you are playing a big fish that is powerfully taking line. Now, a nicely-made reel with an exposed rim for hand braking makes it possible to apply pressure very firmly but smoothly and to remain confidently in control of the fish. Additional braking pressure applied in any other way tends to be jerky and the increased strain that this puts on the fine leader, not to mention a possibly rather slender hook-hold, is most hazardous. Reels of about three and a half inches diameter are the most suitable and the drum should be wide enough to accommodate twenty-five or fifty yards of backing in addition to the rather bulky fly line. And, needless to say, the lighter the reel the better.

The most useful method of fastening the line to the backing is to whip a small loop at the end of the fly line and a large one – big enough for the reel to pass through – at the end of the backing. The loop in the backing is passed through the loop in the line and then the reel (containing the backing) is passed through this loop in the backing and the two loops are drawn together to make a neat knot.

The two can easily be separated when a change of line is wanted. At the business end of the fly line the leader can be attached by a figure-of-eight knot. This is very convenient and serviceable but some anglers complain that it causes a small bow wave on the surface when the water is smooth if certain manoeuvres, such as working a nymph, are employed. Their answer to the problem is to attach a thick piece of nylon to the line by the use of a needle knot, and then use a blood knot to join the leader to the now permanent piece of thick nylon.

120

The needle knot certainly does reduce the tendency to make a bow wave, but it does make the tip of the line more prone to sinking. This may not affect the way the fly and the leader float while the fish is being covered, but when the line is withdrawn in preparation for a further cast the needle knot can cause the leader and the fly to be drawn beneath the surface, thus causing unwanted wetting of the artificial. This happens especially when one does not want to waste time drying and re-oiling the fly and, therefore, for the purpose of this primary role the figure-of-eight knot would seem to be best. For attaching flies, the knots in common use are the double turl and the tucked half-blood. The latter is the easier to tie, but the double turl is the least obtrusive.

Armed with these basic ideas governing the outfit required, we can now look more fully into the different aspects of dry-fly fishing resulting from variations in the type of water and the species to be sought. Only the brown trout of the chalk-stream has been mentioned more than casually so far, but the rainbow trout, the sea-trout, the grayling, and the brown trout of the rain-fed river may each be the candidate to be offered the floating fly on the running water during the course of the year.

The broad principles to be observed remain the same for all species, but sometimes it is good policy to employ slight variations in tactics which are made necessary by the difference in the habits of the fish. As we have said, the feeding brown trout stations itself suitably close to the surface to intercept the maximum number of flies with the minimum of effort. The sea-trout and grayling never do this. They always lie very close indeed to the bottom and make a separate journey for each fly they take from the surface. And – different again – the rainbow trout appears to observe no self-imposed rules which could be restrictive to its freedom of action. Its behaviour may be like any one of the others, but equally well it may be entirely different and may include some quite startling performances, such as making a surprise appearance at great speed from some unseen position, attacking the fly viciously and then charging off across the top of the water like a show-off that feels very pleased with how clever it has been. Indeed, to enjoy to the full the entertainment provided by the rainbow trout there are times when one must take a very light-hearted view and see the funny side of the fish having the upper hand.

The fact that brown trout feeding on the surface always do so from relatively close quarters is a matter of considerable influence in several respects. In the first place – which is apparently the intention – only a small, unhurried, movement is required to scoop in the fly and, in keeping with the action up to that point, the closing of the mouth is similarly unhurried.

In a fast flow the whole sequence is naturally performed more quickly but in sluggish water the action can be very slow. Of course, the rise of the fish is very exciting and it is not easy, particularly for the novice, to restrain himself from striking too quickly. But the attempt to set the hook must not be timed to occur before the mouth of the fish is properly closed and this involves what can seem to be a very lengthy delay. However, no standard timing can be prescribed and it is just as possible to be too slow as too quick, since the trout usually wastes no time in spitting the artificial out after his jaws have closed on it. Clearly, the correct drill is to watch the movements of the trout carefully and to react accordingly. This is fortunately not as difficult as it may sound after a bit of experience.

On the not-so-frequent occasions when sea-trout or grayling can be caught on the dry fly in very shallow water, their movements are much the same as those of the brown trout and the striking policy should be the same. Much more commonly, however, the fish will rise through two or three feet of water or more to intercept the artificial. It is quite a speedy movement up to the surface and back again, even in a steady flow, and the turn that is made at the surface and the seizure of the fly are both executed quickly. Consequently the strike usually has to be made instantly if the fish is to be hooked successfully. This, of course, relates to the small dry flies we have so far been discussing. With large flies at dusk, or when a stiff breeze is ruffling the surface, the sea-trout requires more time to get its mouth closed properly and then, of course, the strike must be suitably delayed. Rainbow trout are also capable of being extremely quick in ejecting the artificial and, as with grayling, there are times when there is little doubt that the rising fish has no intention of doing more than give the fly a very rapid nip, as opposed to taking it fully into the mouth. Then the only slight chance of hooking the fish depends on the strike being made extremely quickly. It so happens, though, that when the fish – both rainbow trout and grayling – are in the mood simply to challenge the fly, so to speak, they are usually inclined to repeat the action several times at close intervals and then sometimes take too clumsily to avoid getting hooked.

Normally if a brown trout fails to secure the artificial the first time it rises to it, it will not subsequently make more than one further effort to get it, although the fish has not been otherwise disturbed. It seems that two abortive attempts are almost always enough to satisfy the trout that the artificial is not, in fact, a desirable item. However, after the lapse of a further quarter of an hour or so, the trout may possibly make another and more determined effort to seize the artificial, especially if it has consumed quite a few naturals in the meantime. But, generally speaking, it is the first encounter of the day that invariably offers the angler the best prospect of a really solid take on the line.

In steadily flowing water both brown trout and rainbow trout will sometimes approach to within a fraction of an inch of the floating artificial to examine it and then drift down alongside it with the current to maintain this very close scrutiny. This may well be repeated several times and after such inspections one would think that the fish could not possibly fall for the deception. On the contrary, however, it is not at all unusual for the trout to eventually open its mouth quite unhurriedly and to suck in the fly with utter deliberation. When grayling are smutting and are offered a sizeable fly, they will some-times do a little bit of the close inspection routine but this is not really characteristic of them. What is typical of grayling performance, however, is to let the dry fly drift quite a long way past (as much as a yard or two downstream) and then, as if prompted by an afterthought, to make a quick turn, chase after the fly and take it very positively. Brown trout and rainbows will occasionally chase the fly in a similar manner, but this does not happen as nearly as often as with the grayling.

These idiosyncrasies of the different species must always be considered both in respect of the point where one attempts to place the artificial relative to the position of the fish in the first place, and the distance it should be allowed to travel beyond the lie. Also it must be borne in mind that it is much easier to get the fly to drift nicely without drag for a short distance than for a longer one. Therefore, with a brown trout, and knowing that it does not take it long to move the short distance to make the interception, one does not normally attempt to place the fly more than about one foot ahead of the fish and then, if there is no rise, the artificial is lifted off the water when it is about one foot past the fish, hopefully before any drag has become at all pronounced and without any unnecessary wetting of the fly. If a bit of error results in the fly alighting closer to the trout, it should not put it off if it is well on the feed. Indeed, on those occasions when it proves exceedingly difficult to find a pattern that will deceive the trout when presented in the normal way, it may well be that the only chance of success will be to drop the artificial vertically above the nose of the fish. If this tactic succeeds, the trout usually takes the artificial immediately it touches the water and without it having had the chance of making any kind of real inspection. Occasionally rainbow trout can also be hooked by this means but, needless to say, it does not apply with sea-trout or grayling during the daytime when they are lying in relatively deep water. Of course, if a sea-trout is in very shallow water at dusk, a well-aimed dry sedge may be taken instantly. Indeed, this happens so quickly as to suggest that the impulse to seize the fly had occurred before it actually reached the surface of the water below which the trout was waiting.

In addition to the peculiarities mentioned so far, all species of game fish are subject to moods of selectivity, or the lack of it, ranging from being quite uncatchable on any artificial fly on some occasions, to being quite indifferent to the details of the dressings they are willing to take at other times. There never appears to be any apparently logical explanation when either of the two extreme types of behaviour is met but, fortunately, they do not happen so frequently as to cause any more than a healthy amount of alternating doubt and confidence on the part of the angler. Much more commonly the fish are just moderately selective – willing to take a small variety of those patterns thought to be appropriate for the circumstances, but quite uninterested in anything out of keeping with the general appearance of the successful category.

This question is not, of course, confined to the floating fly and, although it is common in some degree to all game fish, it cannot be dealt with more than casually in a general context. Furthermore, while it is related in some respects to that notorious old challenge of 'Does the pattern matter?', some of the answers to the one do not necessarily apply to the other. Therefore, both these ever-recurring problems are dealt with under several of the different headings that follow. Meantime, the broad picture of dry-fly fishing needs to be completed.

Trout can be caught on the floating fly as early as the beginning of March in those areas where the season opens then. But in the main, dry-fly fishing does not get properly under way in reasonably seasonable times until about the middle of April. The most productive period is likely to be between eleven o'clock in the morning until around four o'clock in the afternoon. The large spring olive dun and the darker variety of the medium olives will be the most interesting naturals and any of the popular patterns representing them should be worth a trial. When the warmer weather of May gets established sport may start earlier in the morning and continue throughout the evening, perhaps culminating in a hectic rise to a fall of spinners. But at this time of year – and henceforth – there is likely to be a very quiet spell in the afternoon, say about one o'clock until four, or even five, on a warm day. Now, the paler variety of the medium olive dun will generally be the chief fly, but on the warmer days there may be hatches around lunchtime of pale watery duns, while on cold, windy days the iron blue dun may make a welcome appearance. There is no fly that the trout seem to relish more than the splendid little iron blue, and it is during hatches of this species that the newcomer to fly-fishing is likely to have his most exciting and successful early experiences – encounters to remember for a lifetime.

On those rivers so favoured, the mayfly hatches commence towards the end of May or early in June and last for about a fortnight. It takes a few days for the trout to become accustomed to these apparently huge flies but once feasting starts in earnest it makes a fantastic scene, so much so that in some areas of the country it is the most celebrated event of the year, arousing the enthusiasm even of the non-angling sections of the community. This, of course, is an excellent time to match the wits with any specially large trout known to frequent any particular area and, with the stronger leader that seems to be tolerated by the fish when they are taking the mayfly well, the chances of landing the big specimens are infinitely better than when the small fly and matching leader are being fished.

Although mayfly time assuredly means some very good baskets of trout, if not the best of the season, the fish are not as easy to catch as some hackneyed versions of the 'Duffer's Fortnight' suggest.

Indeed, a variety of frustrating difficulties can arise. It is not uncommon for there to be a spell of several hours during which just an occasional one of the many natural duns drifting down the river is taken by a fish and it seems quite impossible to get an offer to any pattern of artificial. But whatever the reason may be, this usually gives way eventually to a rather dramatic change – bold, solid takes in quick succession to just the same kind of offerings that had been previously ignored. Another common type of experience is to get a lot of irritable-looking nudges at the artificial and some seemingly complete takes, but find it is impossible to get a hook-hold of any sort. The mayfly being such a large object relatively, it is generally accepted policy that the fish should be given plenty of time – considerably more than with the small flies – before tightening. But no matter how long the strike is delayed when the trout are in this mood of apparent hesitation, the artificial comes away with seemingly no resistance. Once again, however, good sport is usually not very far away when the nudging game is in progress.

The artificial mayfly is the best subject for consideration of the matter of fly floatants. There are several kinds of liquid preparations on the market but not all of them are suitable for immediate application while actually fishing and few of the others are capable of keeping the popular iceberg floating high on the water.

It should be remembered, of course, that most artificials are light enough to float of their own accord, but require to be reasonably waterproof to prevent moisture being soaked up. Some anglers prefer not to use any floatant and rely on drying the fly by means of false casting. One particularly good method is to melt a little silicone line grease on the end of the finger and stroke this onto the hackles or hair of the fly. The same grease can be used on the leader but care should be taken to ensure that there is no more than the absolute minimum on the point section so that it does not make too obvious a trough in the skin of the water.

For some time after the end of the mayfly period the river tends to be very quiet indeed with the trout showing an almost complete lack of interest in food of any sort. It is sometimes said that this is because the fish have had such good feeding that they have to become quite hungry before recovering interest in the small flies. But a similar quiet period can happen at this time of the year on streams which lack hatches of mayfly, including many of the rain-fed rivers. In some such places it is believed that the fish are then gorging during the night on the large stonefly, which is a nocturnal creature. This may be so, but it seems equally possible that the middle days of June simply mark the time when, in seasonable conditions, the trout generally become more inclined to be nocturnal than diurnal in their habits. Certainly night fishing can be very good, particularly when the water is at a rather low level.

Now the blue-winged olive may be the most important of the duns that could be on the trout's menu. During flush hatches in the late evening, the fish feed very greedily indeed and the famous kidney-shaped rises can be seen all over the river. It is, however, a notorious fact that at such times when the trout appear to be guzzling up the naturals with complete abandon, they are capable of being so utterly selective that the most skilful and experienced anglers cannot get a single offer. It is not easy to force oneself to depart from the scene of such activity, but when the great difficulty is met the best chance of finding a candidate for the basket is when a feeding fish can be spotted in an area where only a few straggling duns are passing over the lie. Such trout can usually be interested in either an imitation dun or a Sherry Spinner.

It is also at this time of year when opportunities to catch sea-trout on the dry fly begin to appear. Even in the middle of the day, especially when there is a hatch of pale watery duns, fish lying in deep holes under steep banks or overhanging trees will sometimes rise and feed on the surface and, significantly, they will probably make no more disturbance than a tiny dimple. The whole event may pass unnoticed unless the angler knows just what he is looking for.

However, the sport then to be had with a lusty sea-trout on a very small fly and a fine leader is something to be remembered. The period around dusk does, of course, offer the most reliable prospects and a variety of dun and sedge patterns may be successful, although one should not be surprised to find the sea-trout behaving very selectively, especially when there are lots of blue-winged olives about.

Daytime sport with the brown trout usually remains quite difficult throughout July, and August can be a particularly poor month. A spell of wet weather may create some interesting opportunities, but usually if one has the alternative of some sea-trout fishing it is by far the more attractive proposition.

September can be expected to bring a considerable improvement in the amount of fly to be seen during the daytime and the degree of interest shown by the brown trout and rainbows. Also the grayling should now be getting into sufficiently good trim to compete for the attention of the angler. Indeed, sport with the grayling on the same standard patterns of dry flies that would be used for the trout can be so good that many anglers find it to be the most attractive because a lot of the trout are then heavy in spawn. The rainbow, of course, will remain in the height of good condition for another month or so and provide most interesting fishing for as long as the law in the particular area allows.

For the rest of the autumn, on the days when there are good hatches of fly, dry patterns representing some form of the natural are to be recommended for the grayling. In the absence of naturals, however, it will probably be found that the fancy grayling patterns such as the Grayling Steel Blue, Red Tag, and the various bumbles, will attract more response than the more sober-looking trout flies.

Even in November and December there are days when the dry fly will do very well with the grayling, and the fight of the fish can be very exciting. Undoubtedly the wet fly is generally more reliable during the late autumn and winter, particularly towards dusk, when there is rarely a day the water is in a reasonable condition that does not offer some promise of response to the floating fly. And by the time the grayling must be rested because of the approach of the spawning season, the dry-fly fisher is again commencing his encounters with the brown trout.

Chapter 24

The Fly Matters

A two-pound chalk stream trout rises as if to take your fly. He hesitates; he makes a long and very close inspection. Then he decides against acceptance and gently drops back to his lie. All sorts of intricate thoughts rush through your mind, but it is the simplest interpretation that reveals the basis for progressive investigation.

First, there is the question of presentation; the trout has shown that this has been performed tolerably well. The fly itself then, must finally have been responsible for the failure. Yet at the range at which the artificial had to make its first impact and arouse the trout's further interest, it proved to have enough appeal to prompt a closer examination. It can be assumed, therefore, that the shortcomings of the fly were more in the nature of detail than of overall appearance. What better proof could you have of the extent to which the fly does matter – both in respect of the pattern generally and its specific dressing?

Such an experience came my way during one of the occasions in the summer when I was at Foston Beck as a guest of Arthur Oglesby. Occasional specimens of a variety of flies had been appearing on the water, and I had shown the fish in question a fairly comprehensive selection of artificials – Pale Watery duns (including J.W. Dunne's type of dressing), B.W.O. dun, Sherry Spinner, Tups Indispensable (dry of course), Black Gnat, Knotted Midge etc. – all had been completely ignored. With polaroid glasses, I could see the shadow of the trout better than the fish itself, but there was no doubt that it had never moved an inch. Then, rather in desperation, I put on a John Storey – the principal one of the few patterns that Arthur Oglesby would be willing to rely upon to the exclusion of all others – and it was when this floated over the trout that he came up to examine it at the point of his nose. Repeated offerings of the same fly, however, aroused no further response at that time. Feeling slightly encouraged, I changed again and tried another variety of fly. Two or three times the fish moved aside as the fly approached, but that was all that happened.

Eventually, I mounted the John Storey again – more, I should say, in desperation than in hope – and I was quite surprised when the trout came up to make a close inspection as before. The full sequence of events as previously described was repeated several times, and on each occasion when the John Storey made a fresh appearance after a spell with other flies, the trout came and gave it a very thorough examination. Finally, to my utter astonishment, he again came up close to the John Storey, drifted down the current in front of the fly for about a couple of feet, and then sucked it in as casually as could be.

I hate to have to say that my reaction was a ridiculous snatch that just pricked the fish, and that was the end of the affair.

Although in that instance the fancy pattern scored over the attempts at imitation of naturals, it was nevertheless convincing proof that the fly really did matter.

But the occurrence must have some deeper meaning that is worth studying. We know well enough that there are many occasions when the imitations of the naturals kill many fish in all sorts of circumstances. Also we know that there are times when the trout will ignore the natural dun itself. Therefore, any lack of interest in the imitation does not necessarily mean that it has failed to simulate the natural. For those same reasons, it would offer no solution to suggest that the fancy fly might create, to the eye of the trout, a superior illusion of the natural dun. Therefore, it must be assumed that in some circumstances the reason why the fancy fly is taken is because it is different from the natural duns and their imitations.

There can be no doubt, of course, that the trout thinks the fancy fly to be food in the form of some small living creature. And many anglers are understandably of the opinion that the John Storey and several of the other patterns that share the brown hackle and peacock herl body are taken for land flies. These, being a less familiar sight to the trout than duns, are thought to evoke curiosity at times when the fish are not in a very active feeding humour.

Another line of thought is possibly nearer the truth in many cases when the fancy fly does better than the orthodox imitations. A hatch of duns almost invariably excites the most voracious response from the trout because nymphs in eclosion are such easy prey and provide great feasts with the minimum of effort for the fish. Consequently it is reasonable to assume that the hatching dun has more fundamental and compelling appeal for the trout than the river fly in any other form. Now, if you watch the contortions of the dun when it is struggling to emerge from its nymphal shuck, it is easy to imagine how some of the suitably-coloured fancy flies could simulate the natural in one stage or another of this performance. It may well be, then, that some of the very effective fancy flies – certainly the John Storey, Treacle Parkin and Grey Duster – are, in fact, not only truer imitations of natural fly food for the trout than most of the artificial duns and spinners, but also simulate the fly in its most desirable form as far as the fish are concerned.

Acceptance of the importance of fly selection, of course, does not depend on agreement with any theoretical argument. Practical fishing nearly always shows that in any particular set of circumstances one certain type of pattern brings more ready response than others. But this fact itself gives rise to another problem, especially for novices. If you look at four John Storeys dressed by four different people, you will probably see four quite different flies. All four may kill well, and each is sure to have its devotees who consider it to be the best dressing. Furthermore, experienced anglers are usually quite open-minded about the potential of dressings that are not in accordance with their own personal ideas. But one important point does emerge. You must have 'the eye for a fly'; you must be able to judge for yourself whether or not it is the sort of creation that is likely to deceive the trout. If you are not confident of yourself in that respect, and you feel tempted to try any fly of which you have no experience, do not rely on suppliers from anonymous sources. And never fail to take advantage of the chance to examine a natural nymph, dun or spinner. Then you will see for yourself how common a fault it is to over-dress flies to a ridiculous degree.

Chapter 25

Wet-fly Fishing

There is a widespread tendency among anglers who have had no personal experience of wet-fly fishing to assume that because dry-fly fishing is such a superlative sport, it follows that wet-fly fishing must be of a less good standing, if not decidedly inferior. Indeed, it is not uncommon for wet-fly fishing to be described as a 'chuck and chance it' method requiring little knowledge or skill.

This is most peculiar because a little research shows that the wet-fly method reached a high degree of efficiency and sophistication in both principle and practice long before any other style of game fishing. It is true to say that some of the very ancient patterns of wet flies of unrecorded origin, which are still used and unsurpassed today, reflect an understanding of entomology and the habits of trout which is considerably more evolved than the level of knowledge required in modern dry-fly fishing. And the degree of manual skill needed in wet-fly fishing is such that the individual will probably find it more difficult to satisfy himself in that regard than when he is using the floating fly.

The wet-fly story starts on a rain-fed river when there is a flush hatch of fly, say large spring olive duns, on a damp, raw and breezy day towards the end of March or early in April. The location will probably be the streamy water towards the head of a pool and in the partial shelter of some trees. It can be seen that the trout are mainly concentrated in a dense group in the area where the duns are emerging the most profusely and each fish is clearly making sure that it gets its full share of the feast while it lasts. The observer cannot fail to notice that all the activity of the fish is very close to the surface and could be forgiven if he thought that their interest was directed exclusively at the fully emerged duns riding on the skin of the water. Of course, a few duns are sure to be taken, but it is the hatching dun struggling to free itself from the nymphal shuck that is the big attraction because it is easier to catch than either the nymph, as it rises quickly through the fast shallow water on its journey from the bottom, or the dun which has succeeded in breaking through the surface skin of the water and is preparing to become airborne.

The famous Waterhen Bloa is a well-proved, old fly pattern representing the emerging dun of the large spring olive, and it will be seen that the angler must attempt to make it drift unchecked with the flow at a level just beneath the surface so that it will simulate the general behaviour of the natural. Now, knowing how quickly drag sets in with the dry-fly, unless all sorts of precautions are taken, it can be judged that if a fairly straight floating line is dropped onto the water at any angle across the current, the slightly submerged artificial fly will be certain to be subjected to some small amount of drag. In the streamy water it can be assumed that this drag will not be steady and even, but varying in strength and intermittent. It is the slight, irregular drag of this sort that makes the hackles of the wet-fly dressing perform the opening and closing motion and thus complete the naturalistic appearance.

It is well documented that in the ancient days of plaited hair lines which were too light to be thrown far, this performance of the wet fly was achieved by fishing more or less directly upstream with a short length of line and an extremely long rod – well into the teens of feet. After each cast, the rod point was continuously raised to keep the line reasonably tight as the team of flies drifted down towards the angler and trout could be hooked at very close quarters indeed. Silkworm gut was used for the cast as it was then called. This had to be soaked in water before use, otherwise it was too stiff and brittle, but having been thus treated it was heavy enough to penetrate the water slightly and fish the flies at the suitable level near the surface without any tendency for them to skim, although the light hair line did not sink at all. With the heavy rods then used this was, of course, very hard work, but nevertheless, as a method, it was excellent in principle and very effective in practice.

Eventually the oil-dressed silk line was introduced. This was quite revolutionary because of the very greatly increased casting potential and it resulted in rapid development in the design of rods to give the improved performance that had to be made possible. The line would not float on its own accord, but the way in which it kept tight onto

133

the flies when used in the traditional upstream manner gave it the correct performance without there being any need for it to be greased. And it is quite wrong to interpret the legendary ungreased line for wet-fly fishing as indicating any intention that it should be a means of fishing the flies deeply. If the modern plastic-coated line is used, it should certainly be the floater, not the sinking variety.

In selecting the equipment, however, it is again necessary to start with the flies and leader. Standard practice is to use three artificials, the point fly and two droppers, but the top dropper is also known as the bob fly. The leader is usually about nine feet long, this being the most manageable and trouble-free length, and the droppers are kept short, no more than about one and a half inches, so that there is less risk of their getting tangled round the main body of the leader. The flies are spaced at intervals of about one yard, and therefore the bob fly is about one yard from the top of the leader. It can be seen that if the leader were tapered as steeply as the one for dry-fly fishing, the bob fly would be attached to very thick, unsightly nylon. Consequently the popular practice is to use fine nylon for the whole of the leader, say four pounds test for big waters early in the season, and three pounds test for more exacting conditions later on.

Needless to say, the finer the line the better from the point of view of balancing the leader, which is really quite delicate for the amount of strain it may have to cope with at times. But there is another factor of great importance which also makes the finest line that one can manage to be the most desirable. When fishing across the current one is often tempted to cast much farther than would be considered suitable for upstream work. Then it is absolutely certain that very soon after the trout has taken the fly, the strain of the pull of the water on the relatively thick line will be felt by the fish through the leader. And unless the angler is very quick indeed, the fly will be spat out before he has had the chance to secure a hook-hold. Of course, the occasional fish will hook itself, and some critics take this to be the basic principle upon which the wet-fly method functions. But the accomplished angler sees it as a failure on his part if a trout does, in fact, succeed in hooking itself. His objective is always to detect the offer and take action to set the hook before the suspicions of the fish have been aroused. Clearly, the thicker the line, the more quickly is the fish likely to become aware of it after intercepting the fly. And in practice, over a period of time, the angler usually finds that his efficiency in hooking the trout is largely governed by the line size.

There is no doubt that an AFTM number four double-tapered floater (AFTM DT4F) offers great advantages over heavier lines and that an AFTM DT6F is the top limit of the range that can generally be considered to be suitable. In silk lines, a number two is the most generally useful and the number three the heaviest to be recommended. But the angler who can be at ease when fishing a number one in all favourable circumstances for sport has the highest degree of efficiency open to him. Normally the silk line will require to be greased to ensure that the flies are fished at the most suitable level near the surface.

The selection of a truly suitable rod is of vital importance. To get the right performance out of the line it must have an adequate amount of through action, yet it must have an element of steeliness in the tip to ensure that it is not necessary to strike very hard in order to hook the fish. Up to a length of about ten feet six inches, the longer the rod, the better it handles and controls the line, and the faster is the movement transferred through the line to the fish when the strike is made. But, as with the selection of the dry-fly rod, one must take into consideration any other duties which it may be desired to perform. If the alternative role of the rod is to be dry-fly and nymph fishing, it is probably wise not to exceed about nine feet, although then it must be recognized that a compromise is, indeed, being made and there will be some sacrifice in respect of the wet-fly performance. On the other hand, if the rod may be required to fish drifts from a boat for stillwater trout the full length of ten feet six inches will be an advantage. The problem of getting the best wet-fly rod is certainly very difficult. One should be very wary of any adviser who does not show a lot of concern for the very special requirements of such a rod. The reel requires to be much the same as for the dry-fly work, about three and a quarter inches, preferably with rim control, and as light as possible.

An essential item of the wet-fly fisher's outfit is some kind of preparation to apply to the leader to remove grease and prevent it from floating. A simple mixture of Fuller's Earth and water with the consistency of thick cream is very effective and quite harmless in all respects. The powder can be obtained from any chemist and, of course, there is nothing more sinister in the word Fuller than that he was an old craftsman engaged in finishing cloth.

Although it is rare to see a wet–fly box that does not contain a big variety of patterns covering all the main types of aquatic flies, the probability is that just a small selection accounts for the big bulk of the season's catch of trout. And while the principal ones may be known by different names in various parts of the country, they are just the same dressings that are most successful everywhere. This is also basically true of the second line of patterns, but here there is sometimes an added complication.

In some districts certain ones of these well-known supporting flies enjoy a specially good reputation and, as a result, they get used so much that they are given an exceptionally good chance to be successful, often at the expense of other, potentially more suitable patterns for certain occasions. Therefore it is not surprising that the records appear to justify the faith placed in those constant favourites. This should be seen by the novice as a warning to avoid becoming unduly prejudiced and to make his trials on a properly planned basis.

Another rather confusing matter with which the novice has to contend is that there appears to be a lot of disagreement among the authors as to the naturals which some of the most popular patterns are supposed to represent. And there are some cases where two apparently opposing views may both be correct because the pattern in question is a reasonably good simulation of more than one species of natural. Therefore, it should be understood that, while recommendations of certain patterns for certain conditions and times of the year can be extremely reliable, statements concerning the purpose for which any particular dressing was originally designed may be no more than arbitrary.

As already indicated, the dressing representing the emergent duns are the principal patterns, but much more use is made of the various species of the other families of water-bred flies than is generally the case in dry-fly fishing. No list of recommendations can be expected to be free from omissions thought to be serious in one quarter or another and the short one that follows is simply a useful selection covering the whole of the season.

The best guide to the amount of dressing that should be used in the tying of the standard patterns is to take a drowned natural, say a Medium Olive Dun or a Dark Needle, place it on the thumb nail, and do likewise with a well wetted artificial. The comparison will show how light the dressing requires to be to simulate the natural.

PATTERN	SIZE	NATURAL	PERIOD
Waterhen Bloa	14	Large Spring Olive	March/April & Sept
" "	16	Small Dark Olive	March/May & Sept
Orange Partridge	14	March Brown	March/May & Sept
Snipe & Purple	16 & 18	Iron Blue Dun	March/June & Sept
February Red	14	Small Stone Fly	March/April
March Brown	12 & 14	March Brown	March & early April
Snipe & Yellow			
Dark Snipe	16	Medium Olive	April/June & Sept
Dark Watchet	16 & 18	Iron Blue Dun	April/June & Sept
Dark Needle	16	Small Stone Fly	April/June & Sept
Brown Owl	16	Small Sedge/Stonefly	April/June
Black Gnat	16	Small Gnat	May/end of season
Poult Bloa	16	Pale Watery Dun	" " " "
Crimson Waterhen	16	Small Red Spinner	" " " "
Knotted Midge	16	Black Midges mating	May/July
Rough Bodied Poult	16	Blue Winged Olive Dun	May/end of season
Green Insect	16 & 18	Aphid	June/end of season

In practical fishing the various factors affecting the decision as to whether one should fish definitely upstream, or across and down, must be given careful and constant consideration. When a lot of trout are feeding close together during a flush hatch of flies and they are, in fact, in such a position that they can be covered adequately by casting more or less straight upstream, there are several good reasons why that is by far the best tactic. Firstly, as the old masters were quick to realise, the presence of the angler below the fish is the least disturbing to them. Secondly, since the strike draws the hook towards the corner of the mouth of the fish, there is much less risk of failing to get a good hook-hold. Thirdly, it is usually possible to draw the hooked trout downstream away from the rest of the feeding fish quite quickly and then play it out where the disturbance will do the least harm.

At this point it should be mentioned that since appearances would suggest to the novice that this could be a glorious opportunity, with the trout feeding so eagerly, to do some dry-fly fishing, the wet fly is by far the most efficient in these circumstances. In the first place, it is extremely difficult in the popply water that is further disturbed by the activity of the trout to keep one's eye on the floating artificial, which, of course, is a basic essential in dry-fly fishing. But if, for the sake of

137

FISHING REFLECTIONS

experiment, one perseveres and succeeds in keeping track of the
floater, the number of offers that come to it compared with the
amount of feverish activity all around is usually very disappointing.
With the wet fly, the end of the line, which is hopefully floating, is
watched carefully and any stoppage or unnatural movement of any
sort is the signal to tighten on the fish smoothly but firmly. And
usually, at times like these, one soon learns how eminently suitable for
the job are the famous old patterns. Indeed, it often happens that offers
come so readily that one spends most of the time during the hatch in
playing trout and hence gets far less practice at actually fishing the fly
than one would expect.

The other circumstances in which it is really essential to fish very
much upstream are when there are exposed rocks dotted about which
would make it almost impossible to cover the lies with casts made
across the stream, and when the fish are feeding in a glide. As we have
said earlier, during flush hatches on rain-fed rivers, the trout seem to
be able to read the signs well enough always to be concentrated in the
areas where the duns are emerging the most profusely and then the
glides are very much neglected. During spinner falls, however,
narrowing fast glides can be expected to provide both the greatest
quantity of food and the easiest to intercept. And, as usual, the best
trout in the area will be in the most lucrative feeding spot. But unless
the cast is made very much upstream the force of the gliding water
sweeps the leader round so quickly that at best the artificials perform
rather unnaturally and will be subject to skimming round uselessly on
the surface.

On days when there is a sparse hatch over a prolonged period, the
trout tend to be well spread out in all the potentially suitable areas.
Then it is very hard work to persevere for a long time with upstream
casting and, furthermore, one cannot cover a satisfactory large area of
water quickly enough. The most promising and least fatiguing tactic is
to cast across and slightly upstream, say thirty degrees above the
square, and allow the flies to drift with the flow until they reach an
angle of between thirty and forty degrees downstream, then make a
fresh cast. In a stream with a very favourable flow the flies will perhaps
fish correctly throughout their travel, but more often there will be
irregularities here and there in the speed of the current and these will
necessitate action to ensure that the flies do not get dragged round too
quickly. This takes the form of what is called 'mending the line' – an

138

invaluable manoeuvre in many styles of fishing. It is simply a matter of lifting part of the line off the water, without disturbing the flies, and replacing it in a position where it will be relieved of the pressure that was causing the drag. A gentle bowling action with the rod gives the most effective and controllable results.

In practice it is usually quite easy to see how the mend should be made. The most frequent need is to make a small upstream mend, and this tends to apply particularly to the period just after the cast has been made, when the line does seem to have a habit of getting ahead of the leader and thus causing drag on the flies. The positive indication of this is the formation of a downstream belly in the line, and the upstream mend makes the correction needed. The rod-tip should follow round, pointing at the same angle as the line while it moves downstream. And as it approaches the lower limits at which it will fish correctly – usually short of about forty-five degrees downstream – the most common tendency is for the leader to start to swing round too quickly. The effective remedy then is to make a small downstream mend. But after travelling a little more, there is no further action that would prevent the line from ultimately reaching the angle at which it would be 'at the dangle'. This is undesirable because any offers that might come would almost certainly be missed, the fish being practically straight downstream of the leader and direction of the strike. Therefore, nicely before such a position arises, the line is smoothly withdrawn and a fresh cast made.

It is no secret that competence in this matter of controlling the line so that the flies fish correctly and at an angle, offering a good chance of a secure hook-hold, is the vital factor in the practical side of wet-fly fishing. It is, of course, the equivalent of the avoidance of drag in dry-fly fishing and, although faults in presentation with the floater are undoubtedly easier to detect, the tell-tale behaviour of the line in wet-fly fishing is a thoroughly reliable guide when it is needed soon enough.

As the season progresses it becomes more difficult to deceive the trout with the wet fly during the daytime and, particularly when the water is on the low side and tending to lack a good enough flow, it is often a much better proposition to resort to the dry fly. A little experience of situations of this kind is all that is necessary to convince one that it is much easier for the trout to detect the falsity of the artificial fully immersed in the water than the floater that has to be

139

viewed through the skin of the water. The refraction and distortion that take place can often make the image of the artificial that is riding high on the hackle points perfectly acceptable to trout that show complete indifference to the wet fly.

When the trout are feeding greedily on spent spinners in the evenings, however, the wet fly comes into its own again. This is very fortunate because during this hectic spell, which may be very short, one does not want to waste time drying and re-oiling dry flies. The trout will undoubtedly take the floater, but the waterlogged artificial fished just slightly beneath the surface is effective and ideally suited to this fishing under pressure, as the late evening rise could be described.

Chapter 26

Nymph Fishing

In waters that are sufficiently alkaline for liberal amounts of aquatic vegetation to thrive, the brown trout, rainbows and grayling do not have to wait for the activity that occurs during hatches of fly if they feel the urge to feed; they can rummage among the weeds and flush out nymphs and shrimps. And it could be said that they become 'nymph-minded'. But on more acid, pebbly, rivers where a bit of thick moss on some of the larger boulders permanently situated in the fast water is the lushest vegetable growth to be found, the fish get very little chance to see nymphs except during hatches. Then, of course, as the wet-fly fisherman knows so well, much more interest is shown in the emerging dun than in the nymph. And no doubt it is for this reason that the modern style of fishing the leaded nymph which can be so effective on the chalk streams and similar waters, rarely has any real success on the weed-free streams.

The technique popularly employed in the chalk streams requires either the dry or wet-fly rod, reel and line, and the same type of steeply tapered leader as used with the dry fly. The weighted artificial nymph (a pheasant tail with copper wire dressing is used almost universally) is mounted and the lower part of the leader is left free from grease so that it will sink readily, but the upper section is well greased. The ungreased length should be a little longer than the estimated depth of water, which will not often be more than three or four feet.

Ideally one should be able to see every detail of the nymph's descent through the water to the point intended just a few inches ahead of the fish and then, after a well-timed twitch with the rod-point, its life-like movement as it rises again and passes over the head of the trout. Of course it is very exciting to watch the reactions of the fish and to see the speed with which it can intercept the nymph.

141

Where practicable it is best to cast as nearly upstream as possible because the nymph then sinks the most quickly and in line with the flow, which makes it very much easier to achieve accuracy in the positioning of the nymph than when the cast is made at an angle to the flow. And so long as all the details can be observed without too much difficulty, no attention need be paid to the leader. But if for any reason the underwater view is obscured, one watches the floating end of the leader and, as a matter of fact, some anglers tie a bit of flue from a white feather to the leader at this point so that it can be seen more easily. Any quick little movement seen at the greased end of the leader on the surface must be assumed to be an offer from a fish and the strike must be made immediately. If nothing has happened by the time it is judged that the nymph has reached the target area on the bottom, the quick little movement is made with the rod-tip to produce the simulation of life-like movement in the nymph. When fishing 'blind', this often proves to be the vital factor, no doubt because the rising of the nymph from the bottom attracts the attention of fish from a greater distance than when it is simply trundling along the gravel or sand on the bottom.

There is no doubt that nymph fishing is a very valuable subsidiary method on the chalk streams. During much of the fishing season the amount of food that is available is so great that inevitably there are long spells on seemingly favourable days when the angler observing the strict dry-fly rules – casting only upstream and only to fish that are seen to be rising – would have no chance of sport at all with sizeable fish. But when upstream nymphing is allowed, one can be most enjoyably occupied for the long hours that would otherwise be rather frustrating, and there can be no criticism of the degree of skill required to catch good fish in this way.

In the circumstances it is not surprising that attempts have been made over the years at fairly frequent intervals to apply nymph-fishing techniques to the less alkaline rivers. Some well-meaning anglers have even gone so far as to design special patterns of nymphs for the rain-fed rivers and success has been claimed for some of the efforts. But the fact that nymph fishing as such has never achieved any popular following on the weed-free rivers is proof enough that it cannot be regarded either as a good substitute for, or alternative to, the conventional wet-fly method. This does not mean to say that nymph patterns will not catch fish: they certainly will when employed in the same way as the standard wet flies but, in general, they have not done well enough to encourage their regular use and have certainly never threatened to usurp the position of the old-established wet-fly dressings in the esteem of experienced anglers.

In recent times there has been a tendency for wet-fly fishing and nymph fishing to be regarded as nothing more than slight variations of the same method – that is, by the non-participants. But it will be seen that, as emphasized earlier, the really effective area to be fished with the wet fly is the upper level, very near to the surface, while the true zone for the nymph is close to the bottom. And the peculiar fact is that in the type of water where the nymph can be really successful, it fills the gap when fish cannot be caught on the dry fly, but it is the dry fly itself that performs this redeeming role on the rain-fed rivers when the wet fly proves to have lost its charm.

Part Four

Grayling

Chapter 27

The Lady of the River

Every year there comes the autumn crop of articles about grayling. It is one of the many unique features of this fish that there seems to be more variation of opinion about it than any other species.

The experienced angler, with his prejudice practically unassailable, glances through these pieces only casually, just to note whether they are 'for' or 'against'. But what of the young enthusiastic novice for whom there are such realms of delight still personally unexplored? How is he to reconcile the disparaging words of men to whom he looks for wisdom, with the beautiful writings of Pritt, who sought to glorify the grayling? And what a sad thing it is when a youngster innocently allows himself to be persuaded to condemn and ignore a fish that could give him endless joy during the long and otherwise drab winter.

It is just as dangerous, of course, to overstate certain aspects of the case for the grayling – thereby creating apparent grounds for justification of the disparagers – as it is to abuse the fish for false reasons.

First, then, let us examine the chief accusations that are commonly heard. The most frequent is that the grayling is an unwanted intruder in the trout-stream because it is a greedy feeder at the expense of the trout. It is also said that it does much damage by eating trout ova.

A very obvious denial of those assertions is given by the fact that any stretch of trout water that contains good healthy grayling, invariably yields trout in excellent condition. But let us look more closely at such waters. The fly-fisher will say that throughout the trout season he is hardly ever conscious of there being any grayling in the stream. He takes good baskets of trout on wet and dry fly and seldom catches a grayling. But immediately after the end of the trout season – so accurately dated – he gets ready response from the grayling to fancy flies, and is only occasionally troubled with trout.

Why, then, should the grayling, who obviously love to feed on fly, almost entirely ignore the lush hatches during the trout season? The answer is very simple indeed. The trout, much as we admire them, are vicious-natured creatures, and the 'lady of the stream', although apparently not very timid of the close presence of the angler on the bank, is very scared of the trout and keeps well out of their way.

Of course, if a river gets grossly overfished and becomes almost denuded of trout before the end of the season, the grayling will then take full advantage of any hatches of fly and will be caught instead of the trout that have disappeared.

Impressive evidence to support this view that the grayling are very much afraid of the trout is not difficult to find. On odd occasions after the end of the trout season, sport with the grayling is interrupted by the trout coming onto the feed for a spell. During that time it is extremely difficult to locate a taking grayling; but, when that is achieved, it is often found that many fish are huddled together in a very restricted area, and good sport can be had until they become too wary.

Later on, in the depths of winter when hectic sport with the grayling to the gilt tail is in progress, a forlorn-looking spawned trout makes its appearance, and the shoal of grayling immediately disperses.

Everybody will agree that the key to the greatest success when trotting for grayling is to find a big shoal. I used to think the secret was to be able to judge correctly the type of current grayling would favour in the particular circumstances of weather and water. Now I think I have learned better. I try to select the swim least likely to contain any trout, and, if I am right, the grayling are there. That is why, I believe, the strong glides are so good for grayling – such water offers no easy lies for trout and the grayling can accumulate there in safety.

Confirmation of this idea is to be had when there is a bold river in the early part of December. The trout are then busy spawning in the small tributaries and the grayling spread out over the whole river. They can be caught from the top to the bottom of every stretch of water that offers them a reasonable lie with the chance of morsels of food drifting by. But this little honeymoon does not last long. As soon as the trout begin to return to the main river, and although they are then relatively very feeble, the big problem with the grayling again becomes that of finding their whereabouts.

As for the grayling seeking out trout ova, I am quite sure that if it happens at all, it is negligible. The grayling quite certainly keep clear of the area when the trout are actually spawning, and once the redds are completed, I think that they are secure against interference by the grayling. I have often seen grayling working very hard for food under the shelving sides of stones, and actually using the force of the current against their bodies and fins to turn flat stones over with their noses, and then collect the caddis larvae. But I have never seen them digging in the gravel, nor have I ever found any trout ova in the stomach of a grayling.

The other principal complaint made against grayling is that it is a poor fighter. It must be conceded that sometimes a proportion of the grayling make very little effort to avoid being drawn into the net, but that is only a small part of the subject which is much more complex than is realised by those who have not had a close acquaintance with these fish. An occasional grayling will fight with something like the same vigour, speed, and change of direction of the trout; but such fish are actually easier to subdue than those that behave in the more normal grayling manner, which is quite peculiar to that species. Assuming that the grayling is below the angler – and it is best with all methods, including dry fly, to fish downstream – the fish uses the hook-hold as a pivot against which to lever his body across the current, in much the same manner as when he turns over a stone with his nose. His twists and whirls transfer the force of the current to the tackle, and if it is a tip-action rod, all its flex is often completely absorbed. Then the sensation of weight is most impressive, and in fast water the strain exerted on the tackle relative to the size of the fish is quite incredible. Unless the temper of the hooks used is very good, they are frequently straightened out or snapped off. One is tempted and sometimes compelled, to give the fish line, but that does not alter the position in any way. If, for any reason, the angler is unable to move down and alter the direction of the pull so that it is less in line with the current, he requires more skill to land grayling than is ever required to beat a trout of similar size.

Where the circumstances are in favour of these remarkable peculiarities of the grayling, his gameness simply cannot be disputed. Once the angler has experienced this most enjoyable fishing, he is safe for ever against those who would have him regard the grayling as being unworthy of his attention.

149

Is this question of the way a fish fights, though, the all-important factor in the appeal that fishing has for us? In the early days of a fishing career, a great battle with a fish makes a deep impression, and, as time goes along, the fish don't seem to fight as hard or as long as they used to do. Then gradually it is realised that the increasing skill is responsible for this apparent change; and, from that time onwards, the playing of a fish cannot ever be the same thrill that it originally was. But however many seasons one can look back on, the moment of the take of the fish never loses any of its charm. The most enjoyable days – the ones when time passes by with alarming rapidity – are those that are packed full of incidents. It is in that respect that the greatest claim for the grayling can be made. On any reasonable day for the dry fly, more interest is provided per fish caught than with any other species.

When a grayling has been located it is not at all unusual to float the fly over him four or five times before his curiosity is aroused sufficiently to make him move to it. Then at successive casts, he will make a close inspection without touching it, nudge it several times and, apparently, take the fly but give no chance to hook him. Finally he comes up and takes the fly with the maximum of boldness, which makes his previous caution seem all the more a puzzle. But it is all absorbingly entertaining and altogether too good to be missed.

Added to the sport, there is the beauty of the grayling, both shape and colour, the unique, pleasant smell of the fish when he is freshly out of the water. That is particularly noteworthy on a frosty day; there are very few grayling fishers who are not appreciative of it.

If there are any anglers who cannot be reached by the appeal of the grayling on its sporting merits, they must nevertheless acknowledge that this fish is a blessing in another way. Trout can thrive in water which is much more polluted than grayling can tolerate. Therefore, so long as the stream is inhabited by some native healthy young grayling, the angler need have no fears for his trout. And when the grayling begin to disappear, as they unhappily are doing in some waters that have deteriorated in purity in recent years, it is time seriously to investigate the position even though the trout do not yet appear to be suffering. It will surely be their turn next.

Finally, I regularly have a grilled grayling on my return from the river. After a day's trout fishing, I invariably give my catch to my friends.

Chapter 28

A Case of Sunshine and Bradshaw's Fancy

It was a lovely cloudless mid-November day – warm in the sunshine, but noticeably cool in the shade. The river was high and still rising when we arrived. The colour suggested surface washings, and we judged that the grayling would not be very interested until that phase had passed.

Wisely Herbert Normington was prepared for either fly or trotting the gilt-tail, and, needless to say, it was his float that was sent off in search of a grayling. Soon, very close to the bank, it dipped, and for him a blank day at least was averted. We wondered if, after all, our assessment of the conditions was wrong, whether the grayling were indeed in a feeding mood. But this optimism did not last long. The gilt-tail went down the stream again time after time, but was completely ignored.

Relying solely on fly until the weather becomes really arctic as I do, I was keeping a watch for rises; even in such circumstances, I expected to see the odd ones close to the bank. But nothing disturbed the unruffled surface. I made a few heartless casts and then had lunch.

The sun was behind us, and even at one o' clock the steepness of the valley caused our bank to be shaded. I told Herbert that I would take the footbridge and try a favourite place on the other side. If there was nothing doing there, I would give the grayling best for that day. While crossing to the sun-bathed bank, I saw an expanding ring on the smooth fast glide. It pinpointed a grayling close to the edge and alongside a projecting and partially submerged tuft of grass. No natural fly was to be seen on the water and I assumed that what the grayling had taken had fallen from the overhanging trees.

Land flies are usually much more substantial that the wet-flies then on my cast – Orange Partridge and Tinsel, Dark Needle, and at the

151

bob a Snipe and Purple in lieu of a Fog Black – and consequently I looked for something rather more meaty. The Red Tags were there, of course, but a solitary Bradshaw's Fancy had lain in my box of grayling flies for many years without my ever being tempted to try it. It struck me that the double daub of red might help, in view of the colour and speed of the current. At the same time, though, I thought the colour was improving slightly. Nevertheless, I put on the Bradshaw's Fancy in place of the Dark Needle.

A big bulging rise close to the grass marker was the cheering response to my first cast, and I tightened. The grayling fought splendidly – very different from those of a few days ago when the river was low and the weather muggy – and when he was in the net, it was quite a delight to see that it was the Bradshaw's Fancy that had done the trick.

Ready to cast again, I looked around and spotted another rise thirty yards below. The Bradshaw took that fish at the first cast too. Then, in approximately the same spot, I lost a nice grayling and missed another offer. Thinking that the disturbance would have put those fish down for a while, I sauntered up until I was opposite Herbert. He had seen the activity with the fly, but his worm was still being ignored.

While chatting across the water, a bulge occurred practically at my feet. I cast and within seconds I was actually having to give line to a grayling! Two more followed that one into the net in a remarkably short time and Herbert made some comments about gilt-tails that were heartfelt whether or not they were merited.

A little higher up I missed another grayling, lost one, and added number six to the credit of the Bradshaw – every one taken from close under the bank. Then, missing a good rise and anxious to give that fish another chance, I forgot that a roll-cast was needed and finished up with the cast entangled in a tree and completely out of reach.

I do not know if it was the loss of the Bradshaw's Fancy that was responsible, or if it was the way the temperature dived as the sun went behind the hills, but I saw no more rises and could not get another offer. Meantime, Herbert was enjoying a welcome but short burst of activity, and landed three more fine fighting grayling. Then mist started to rise from the water and our day was done.

We saw no other rods on the river and I was rather glad because I would have been thought to be foolishly stubborn for fishing fly with a water like that. However, the events of the afternoon seemed to support my belief that sunshine has a very good influence on grayling. And I added to my collection of mental pictures of special tactics for special conditions.

Very probably a variety of other patterns would have been accepted equally well by the grayling. But if one dressing serves gratifyingly well, why look for another? Certainly I shall see to it that henceforth my grayling fly-box will never be without its complement of Bradshaw's Fancies.

Chapter 29

Confessions of a Fly Dresser

No doubt you will agree that already there are far too many patterns of artificial flies for grayling, also for salmon, sea-trout and brown trout. But it tends to be an occupational disease among fly tyers to indulge in creating patterns of their own, and were it not for the fact that other anglers are harder to convince of the merits of the new efforts than the inventors themselves, the list of recognized patterns would keep on growing at an alarming rate.

I was very conscious of this sobering thought when I felt the need for a new kind of dressing. Having tied up the fly, tried it, and asked two or three friends to try it, I decided to keep quiet about it and just retain it for the use of close friends and myself.

Then a remarkable report came first from one and then the others of my friends, and now it is clear that I must tell the whole story or have it appear that I am trying to keep something up my sleeve.

To start with I should say that two of my favourite grayling flies are Sturdy's Fancy – originally designed as a spinner pattern – and Bradshaw's Fancy. I don't know what the latter is supposed to represent, but I use it as a wet fly when I want a meaty-looking pattern to make a lot of impact. And the grayling show a great liking for it on occasions.

Next I should say that just about my favourite sea-trout fly is the Claret & Mallard. When wet, the claret body with gold ribbing poses what one imagines must be a very appetising appearance to the fish, suggestive of a spinner's abdomen.

It struck me that with elements of these patterns, plus a little something from the Treacle Parkin – another very successful fly – a dressing could be formulated which would fill the need I felt for a very succulent spinner to be used wet. So, I tied up the pattern as follows:-

154

Hook: Captain Hamilton (Partridge) L2A
           size 16.
Hackle: Hooded Crow, as per Bradshaw's
           Fancy.
Body: Mixed claret rabbit & claret polar
           bear, ribbed gold twist.
Tag: Orangey yellow as Treacle Parkin.

When well soaked I thought this would look to the fish like some kind of pregnant spinner, the tag being the eggs.

The first time I tried it was on the Eden where I was a guest on a complimentary ticket for trout and grayling. There were some grayling dimpling in a nice glide and very soon I hooked and landed a good one with the new fly, which was on the point. A few casts later it was taken with a beautiful head-and-tail rise and a glimpse of the dorsal fin made me think that I was into a really monster grayling. Soon, however, I realized that it was a little cock salmon of about eight pounds which was rather red. Normally I would have lowered the rod and jerked to break off and leave the fly in the fish, but as it happened I was trying out a prototype eight and a half foot Hexagraph rod and wanted to see just how it would perform, although with three pound nylon at the point I could not use a great deal of pressure. The salmon made a few good runs and each time I brought it back and close in. Then suddenly and much to my surprise, it sidled towards me in the very shallow water and went right onto its side at my feet for a moment. I bent down, twitched to remove the fly but broke it off and away went the salmon with bags of steam still left in it.

This very satisfactory incident got me thinking. The name of the pattern came to me – the Salmon Approved Grayling Enticer, The SAGE Fly.

Soon Neville Gilder told me an amazing story about fishing the Annan with the Sage Fly on a three-fly cast. He had a large number of grayling on the Sage Fly, but only two or three parr on the others. Then John Winter told me that he had done well with the Wear grayling on the new pattern.

More recently I heard from Michael Powell, the retired parson son of the late Rev. Edward Powell, the famous inventor of many very popular patterns including the Orange Otter, widely recognized to be an exceptionally good grayling fly. I will not repeat what Michael said

155

of the Sage Fly in comparison to the Orange Otter, but I will say that his enthusiasm for it is such that I have felt compelled to make a full confession and introduce the Sage Fly to the members of The Grayling Society.

Chapter 30

The Grayling Rise

Brian Morland's article on the intriguing subject of 'The Grayling Rise' in the Spring 1979 issue of the *Grayling Society Newsletter* immediately got me 'rising' too.

I agree of course with most of what he said on this complex phenomenon and I thoroughly enjoyed the way in which he approached it and put his ideas over, but I think there are some other factors of vital importance which should have been taken into consideration.

First, there is the position of the mouth of the grayling. It is true that in certain classes of river, the mouth tends to be tucked well underneath – not unlike that of the barbel – but on many of the shallower stony and faster streams, the underslinging is only very slight indeed.

Secondly, the very vertical rise through deepish water to intercept food on the surface is not nearly such an invariable rule as some writers would have us believe. As recently as last autumn on the Test I saw much convincing evidence of this fact. The spot I was fishing was comparatively narrow and in the region of four to five feet deep. The flow was quite fast and swirly, due to some well-positioned weed beds, and the general area was well stocked with beautiful grayling.

After a bit of careful selection regarding the exact spot from which to start casting, I was able to see right down into the water without the use of polarising glasses and therefore without my vision being diminished in any way. Indeed, I was able to watch everything that happened in satisfactory detail.

There was a nice mixed hatch of flies and I was able to watch the whole of lots of rises to the natural as well as those to my floating artificial. And I am sure that there were more approaches to the surface at well slanted angles than those that were close to the vertical.

Indeed, I was very surprised to see how far from the line of travel of the fly some of the grayling came to make their interceptions – as much as four or five yards. And believe me, when they went for the natural, they did not miss.

At this point I must make a deviation from the main theme. As I have said, there was a mixed hatch, and I got a very strong impression that although every kind of fly was being taken by one fish or another – quite greedily too – individually the grayling were being very selective and rising only to one particular variety of natural. And I think this could possibly have accounted for the criss-crossing of the tracks of the rising fish within my field of view. I must acknowledge that this was a possibility that had never occurred to me before and as far as I know, there have never been any suggestions of this sort from any other source. It is certainly a point I shall watch for in the future.

But back to the main point. I believe that the so-called short takes and misses only occur unintentionally in a very small minority of cases, such as when a natural fly takes off just before it would otherwise be seized by a fish. In my opinion, the predominant reason for the misses is that the grayling had no intention from the beginning actually to attempt to seize the artificial and simply meant to give it a tup with the snout and with the mouth closed. But after treating what would seem to the fish to be a succession of similar suspicious items in this aggressive way in a very short space of time, familiarity with the particular image created by the artificial induces the grayling to sample it as a possibly edible morsel. Thus it gets hooked after seeming to have missed the fly several times.

There appears to be some confirmation of this inclination to tup suspicious or intrusive items when the grayling are not very hungry and they are offered a small red worm on trotting tackle. On many occasions I have hooked fish in various places outside the mouth and close to the eye. And it has been my experience that on those occasions when this happens once, it tends to occur several times. I personally have no doubt at all that they tup the worm with no intention of taking it.

While on this subject of 'bites' that are not 'bites', so to speak, I should mention another of my beliefs. Not uncommonly while trotting I get what appears to be a very solid offer but when I tighten, there is just a momentary firm resistance and then nothing. When I reel in to examine the tackle, I find the worm to be in perfect order. I always hook gilt-tails or brandlings by the tiniest bit of skin on the head so that they keep on wriggling for a long time, and when I miss a genuine bite, I almost always lose the worm, or at least part of it. And so, when the worm comes back practically untouched despite my having felt definite resistance, I believe it to be because the grayling had taken one of the lead shot and never even touched the worm. Often you find a lot of little snails in the stomachs of grayling that do not look unlike lead shot and I think this taking of the shot is a very frequent occurrence. Indeed, when you think about it, it would be even more remarkable if they did not take the shot on occasions.

Chapter 31

Making a Grayling-float

'It is only the worm fisher who has played a well-matured December grayling who knows the gameness and strength of the fish, and, at the same time, has the opportunity of testing his most excellent edible flavour.' So said T.E.Pritt in his delightful *Book of the Grayling* published in 1888.

These were the words, it will be known, of a great fly fisher. And like many of his counterparts of today, not until the rigours of winter compelled the laying aside of the fly-rod did he resort to the float and the worm. But all who are familiar with trotting the gilt tail or brandling will confirm that the fascination of the float sailing down the current is an instant cure for the sadness that is felt when the time comes for the fly tackle to have its two or three months rest.

The cob-float held sway in Pritt's day and there have been very few serious challenges to its long supremacy. But the variety of designs that have been tried out from time to time reveals the desirable features that are sacrificed in the cob.

Let us then consider the principal requirements. Sufficient weight is needed to enable a long enough cast to be made with an under-hand lob so gentle that the lightly hooked worm will not be thrown off. And during its flight, the float must turn over smoothly, positively, and once only, in order to avoid the annoying tendency, as with quills, to get caught up and reversed on the line. If that happens, either it remains flat on the water, or swims upside-down.

There must be sufficient buoyancy to ride rough currents without underwater eddies sucking the float under. And enough lateral water resistance must be exerted to permit efficient mending of the line, and to draw the line along for a suitable distance downstream without checking the free travel of the float.

Yet despite the buoyancy, the float must be so sensitive as to reveal every touch by a grayling. Furthermore, it must be easy to see for up to fifty yards. And during its rapid recovery it must not cause a lot of commotion on the water as the cob does.

I will not pretend that I had any expectations of fulfilling all the requirements when I started my experimental float-making many years ago. And it must be acknowledged that it was a totally wrong conception – one of my innumerable failures – that actually gave me the clue to the origination of a surprisingly efficient answer to the problem. It has been none-the-less pleasing, however, to see the final model gaining popularity during the last few seasons; and now it is firmly in favour with several of the most successful grayling fishers in upper Wharfedale.

The float is not obtainable commercially and must be made by the individual. But the cost of the necessary materials is negligible and with a little practice completely serviceable floats can be produced by anyone.

From a three-eighths-inch square stick of balsa wood, procurable at the handicrafts shop, cut a length of about three and a half inches – Fig. 6.1. With a sharp knife and fine sandpaper shape the soft wood as in Fig. 6.2. Take a four and a half inch length of twenty gauge piano wire – Fig. 6.3. Hold this vertically between the forefinger and thumb of the left hand leaving one inch clear at the top and place the other end on a hard surface. Take the balsa wood body in the right hand and press it down on the wire until the base of the body is touching the point of grip of the left hand – Fig. 6.4. Now whittle the base of the balsa wood flush with the wire – Fig. 6.5. Whip on the fine wire loop at the bottom of the float and it is ready for painting.

Cellulose paint is very suitable and gives a very durable finish. First apply an undercoat of white. When this has dried, in a few minutes, it will be seen that the balsa wood has a tendency to be whiskery. Rub smooth with a fine sandpaper and further trouble in this respect will not be experienced with subsequent coats of paint.

After application of the final coat, allow the float to stand overnight. Then the paint will be hard enough to take the rubber float cap without marking.

It will be found that the float is self-cocking. One large shot will submerge it correctly so that only the antenna protrudes.

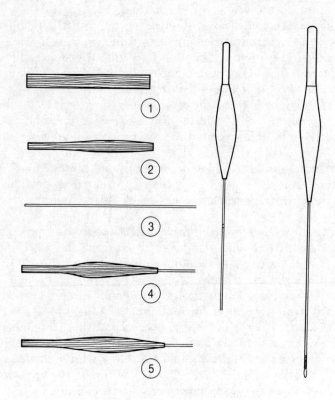

HOW TO MAKE THE BALSA FLOAT

The long wire base of the float acts as an extremely efficient keel and keeps the antenna vertical despite rough water and wind. And although the mechanics – or is it the physics? – of the problem are still a puzzle to me, it so happens that the opposing requirements of buoyancy to cope with rough water and sensitiveness to register every offer from a grayling are fulfilled remarkably well. A fish has only to stop the bait, and the float goes straight under. Often a cob float simply halts in its tracks or moves a little sideways when a grayling takes, and there are many occurrences which cause doubt. No indecision arises with the balsa float.

Some time ago, a very well-known fly fisher, who had previously had little experience of trotting for grayling, was one of my guests on the Wharfe. In no time at all he was able to swim the balsa float as far as he ever wished. He mended his line without affecting the progress of the float, and was elated when very soon he hooked a grayling at what he considered to be a remarkable distance. The relative position of the tree on the bank enabled us to pace it out quite accurately – seventy yards! But he, Terry Thomas, acknowledged that that was nowhere near the limit.

Meantime a little higher upstream, my other guest, on his first visit to the Wharfe, was having an extremely busy time landing grayling one after the other in quick succession. Need I say that that was Bernard Venables testing the balsa float.

My use of the balsa float has been restricted to trotting for grayling, but friends tell me that it behaves just as well for other species in both still and running water.

In case the ungainly appearance of the float should cause any doubts, let me say that even in very shallow crystal-clear water it does not seem to worry the grayling provided that it is allowed to travel at the full pace of the stream. I fondly imagine that the fish pays no attention to it because they take it to be a leaf floating stem downwards.

The story would not be complete without commenting on the fact that several anglers who have adopted the balsa float have produced modifications of their own, such as a shorter wire or more bulbous body, but I do urge reasonable adherence to the relative proportions shown here.

Chapter 32

Trotting the Gilt-tail

Until comparatively recently – well within living memory – some of the celebrated grayling fishers in the Yorkshire Dales used their fly rods, and reels and lines for trotting the gilt-tail. The method was to cast the cob float into the stream and walk along the bank abreast of it. And, even today, with modern float tackle, there are still a few anglers who prefer this way of fishing.

Of course it has its limitations in covering pools adequately; it is, usually, wasteful of good fishing water. But it does account for some fine baskets of grayling and, in very cold weather, has an appealing advantage. Gloves can be worn with a minimum of inconvenience, and the continuous gentle exercise does prevent too great discomfort.

'Fine and far off' devotees will think this to be a very primitive system. Yet the choice of equipment of such anglers – who think themselves fully up-to-date – is far from being the most suitable to give them full mastery of the long trotting method. Admittedly on small streams where the pools are short, any reasonably modern float-fishing tackle will serve tolerably well. But on the largest rivers on which you wish to trot the float as far as the eye can see, there is a need to be extremely selective with every individual item of equipment.

Let us look in detail. The float has been dealt with. It should travel the stream with practically complete freedom from side drag and, therefore, it must be comparatively easy to achieve that. It is necessary to be able to see the line and to correct easily its position on the water relative to the float – to mend the line, in fact. When the float registers a bite at a range of, perhaps, upwards of fifty yards, the strike must lift much of the line off the water instantly and so give almost immediate contact with the fish. Braided Terylene, one and a half pound b.s., is admirable. Braided nylon is the next best, but has a tendency to be too

164

elastic to hook the fish well, and it does not stand up to the hard wear and shock treatment as well as Terylene. Monofilament is quite certainly not suitable. It is often impossible to see it and, consequently, it is only realised that the line needs mending after it has started to impede the float. And the way it clings to the water makes it impossible to make a mend cleanly and without checking the float. That same fault also results in contact being made too slowly when attempting to strike a fish at a long distance.

The choice of rod is not quite as simple as it might seem, because both fly-fishing action and tip action have serious disabilities. The arc through which the rod must move rapidly to hit a distant grayling often finishes well behind the head. This results in the fine line getting entangled round the tip of the rod if there is too much action, as with the fly-rod. The match rod has no difficulty in hooking the grayling of course, but it will be found that a good fish in a strong current will often fight in such a way that all the flex of the fine tip is absorbed; then it is like a rigid piece of wood. The entire strain is borne by the fine tackle and hook-hold; often the fish will be lost, or there will be a breakage.

An eleven-foot, two piece built-cane rod with a reverse taper in the butt – a newcomer to the market – is without doubt the best grayling rod I have ever handled. It fulfils all the requirements admirably, and it is an absolute revelation to feel the fight of a grayling through such a rod – every twist of the fish is felt in a most remarkable way.

If the angler is happiest with a fixed-spool reel, it can be used reasonably well but a good centre-pin is much to be preferred, particularly in cold weather. The fingers of each hand can be kept close together nearly all the time and that saves a lot of discomfort. The rod should be held so that the outer side of the little finger is used as a brake on the rim of the reel. The line is fed by the left hand, using the thumb and forefinger. For recovery, the reel is batted round by the left hand, and that is quicker and easier than reeling in with a fixed-spool reel.

As for the hooks – the temper must be reliable. The grayling's peculiar way of transferring the weight of the current to the tackle is capable of straightening out hooks that will safely bring to the net much bigger specimens of other species. A simple and safe solution is to use the best quality eyed fly hooks. Up-eyed, wide gape, sizes twelve and fourteen will cover most needs.

165

The grayling fisher's esteem for the gilt-tail is very well founded. If it is hooked very lightly close to the back of the head – on the darker side, that is – it will continue to wriggle for a very long time. The movement of the golden coloured tip of the tail is believed to be very attractive to the grayling. But more important perhaps is the fact that the gilt-tail does not seem to be able to stretch itself out like the brandling, and therefore there is less risk on the strike of the point re-entering the worm instead of hooking the fish.

The depth at which the gilt-tail should be fished in relation to the bottom, is an evergreen topic. It is often said that the big secret of some of the great exponents of the past was their complete under-standing of that problem. But there is no need for the inexperienced angler to let the question perplex him. It is obvious that if the float is going to carry the gilt-tail for any considerable distance, there will be many appreciable variations in the depth of water. There cannot be any question then of the float having to be fixed at one precise position. The best policy is to make regular, slight alterations to the length below the float, and thus very soon get an overall picture of the different positions in the swim where the different depths are the most attractive. But anyway, when the grayling are keen on the gilt-tail, they do not mind having to rise quite a long way to take it. Then the only care necessary is to ensure that the worm is clearing the bottom at all points in the swim. Usually it is quite safe to err on the shallow side.

Fly fishers are naturally fully alive to the business of being entirely mobile, but the novice will need to give some thought to it. Varying with the standard of sport, long stretches of river may have to be covered during a day's fishing. It is essential to be able to move from pool to pool without having to gather together your belongings each time a change of position is desirable. Also the lighter you can travel the better, especially since it is to be expected and hoped that your load at the end of the day will be considerably greater than at the beginning – and that the addition is a good basket of grayling.

The newcomer to the sport will probably have acquired concise preconceived ideas about the conditions in which the grayling will show a keen interest. But whatever he may have gleaned from his reading, he should never stay away from the river because it does not seem to be the right sort of day. Splendid sport is often enjoyed in circumstances in which it is least expected. And indeed, the mood of the fish is subject to remarkably sudden changes; a lack of response for even a longish spell should never be considered to be decisive.

One day, a couple of seasons ago, I fished all morning without stirring a fin. After lunch, I returned to a favourite swim which I had tried earlier. Now I took ten grayling – about three-quarters-of-a-pound class each – in ten consecutive casts. The eleventh journey of the float was unproductive, but the twelfth brought another fish to the net. Then I made way for my friend, and soon he too thought that it was a very, very lovely day.

The most commonly experienced happy turn of events, after dull fishing, happens within the last hour of daylight. Then, like so many other fish, the grayling often seem to become relatively incautious, and it is as though they realise that time for feeding for that day is rapidly disappearing. Then anglers who sometimes say that grayling do not fight very well, make the discovery that the gameness of the fish, as the darkness approaches, is the great limiting factor to the size of the catch.

167

Chapter 33

A Case for Fancy Flies

It is generally agreed that when grayling are rising freely to a good hatch of duns, the best policy is to use a pattern which is a suitable imitation of the natural fly. Hence, the Gold Ribbed Hare's Ear would be a fairly popular choice – and most probably a successful one – if the flies in question were medium olives. At the same time, some of the famous grayling patterns, such as the Yellow Bumble, would be pretty certain to attract a lot of attention from the fish.

When plenty of grayling are to be seen feeding, a good selection of potentially productive fishing spots is available. Normally this enables the angler to avoid any sort of background that would make it difficult to see the floating artificial, so there would be no problem in keeping your eye on the most sombre-toned pattern, not even on the popply surface of a North Country stream.

The chalk streams, of course, are greatly favoured in regard to the duration of the hatches of duns in the autumn months. Often there is a more or less continuous light hatch throughout the day and at least some of the grayling are on the go non-stop. You can hardly go wrong with any of the appropriate trout patterns, fished in much the same way as for trout, but tending to allow the artificial quite a lot more drift before it covers the fish, also allowing it to travel considerably further downstream before taking it off the water for the next cast. Frequently grayling show a tendency to let the fly get several feet beyond their lies before deciding to move to it.

In this context, on both the chalk streams and the rain-fed rivers, it is generally agreed that the best ploy is to try and avoid drag just as much as you would when fishing for trout, although it might not be such a critical factor with the grayling.

In contrast to the chalk streams, limestone streams, and the more alkaline of the rain-fed rivers, the stony and practically weed-free streams of the North Country and Scotland tend to have relatively short-lived hatches of duns during the autumn, and on many of the heavily-wooded stretches, such as most of the Derbyshire grayling streams, there are probably more land-bred insects on the water than aquatic flies for the larger part of the day.

Happily, though, the grayling frequently show a willingness at anytime to rise to an isolated item of natural food, or something that could easily be mistaken for such. And with the exception of the occasions when they are busily occupied in smutting, it is very rare for them to show any inclination to be very selective in their feeding.

Now the so-called fancy flies come into their own. They make for highly-efficient fishing and are invaluable. The best chance of getting an offer, of course, is likely to be where a rise has been seen, and the prospects are that there will be at least a small group of fish there. That being so, there is no reason why several grayling should not be taken on the dry artificial from the same stand.

But here comes the crucial point: you have to accept the situation as it is and cope with any difficulties in the way of the light and surface disturbance which may make it difficult to keep sight of the fly. Indeed, the prime factor in choosing the fly is to pick one that is easy to see despite any problem created by the background.

That does not mean to say, though, that the extra impact of a brightish fly with two different strong colours may not have some appeal value to the grayling. There are, in fact, good reasons to believe that on occasions it is a definite advantage to use a pattern which would appear to create a particularly good impact, as will be seen later.

Let us look at a few examples of the exploitation of the fancy-fly principle. Frequently the floating artificial from a brightly shining surface into the shade of a tree. The dark fly that could be seen well against the light background can easily be lost when it enters the very dull area.

But with the Treacle Parkin, for instance, the darkish brown of the hackle and the greeny bronze of the body show up well where the surface is bright, while the glow of the tag can easily be detected against the dark background. Sturdy's Fancy – my personal favourite –

the Grayling Witch, White Witch and Rolt's Witch, are some others which will perform similarly.

On a very bright day when there are very few shaded areas, the Red Tag – the most famous of all fancy grayling flies – is easy to see and is undoubtedly well-liked by the fish. But when the sun is high enough possibly to be dazzling to the grayling, the Grayling Steel Blue – again easy for the angler to see – often does better, perhaps because it creates extra impact.

Another way to increase the impact which can often be useful when there are very few naturals to keep the interest of the grayling keen, is to impart little bits of drag to the artificial. This seems to be particularly successful in glides. Normally grayling will not move far laterally to take any fly, but drag apparently creates enough extra excitement in the fish to induce it to make the greater effort required.

When there is anything more than just a light breeze, the fancy grayling patterns often produce fine sport fished wet – just beneath the surface – particularly when few natural flies are about. There seems no doubt that a pattern with a little bit of gold, silver, or some very bright colour, is more attractive to the grayling than is a sombre-looking fly.

Again, when the days are at their shortest, the water cold, and the angler resorts to the leaded fancy grayling flies fished much deeper than usual, the bright colours, possibly red more so than any other, have proved valuable. Bradshaw's Fancy is a particularly good example, and this pattern also does well earlier in the season when it is fished nearer to the surface in a slightly-coloured water.

In all the situations I have mentioned it could be argued that duller patterns intended to imitate specific species of naturals could be seen easily enough and make sufficient impact, if used in large enough sizes, say fourteen and bigger. But only in the case of leaded flies used in the depths of winter – when the grayling can be very hungry indeed – is it recommended to use anything larger than a sixteen.

It is true that in relatively special circumstances grayling can be caught on bigger flies. Especially is this so on some of the chalk streams where the fish are used to good supplies of naturals of large size. But on most grayling rivers it would be a disservice to the beginner to suggest that he could take much liberty in respect of size.

170

Lightly-dressed size sixteen hooks are as big as he is ever likely to require for dry-fly fishing and often he will do much better with an eighteen. Furthermore, size sixteen and eighteen hold grayling safely if the fish is hooked in the secure area of the top jaw. Larger hooks tear away from the soft parts of the mouth just as easily as the smaller ones do.

Most of us want all the help we can get when fishing, so look at it this way: Supposing a grayling would, in fact, accept a fly tied on a size fourteen, would it ignore a sixteen? It is most unlikely. But when a fish will take a fly on a size sixteen or eighteen freely, they often refuse to accept anything bigger. Countless experiments over the years have proved this to my satisfaction completely. It is also equally true to say that exactly the same thing often happens when fishing dry for trout. This may look a little bit odd until you remember that with most dressings, flies tied on size fourteen hooks are twice the size of those on a sixteen – that is, the fly overall.

What advantage is there, then, in using size fourteen hooks? On most rivers, where a pounder is a good grayling, the beginner in particular should heed this advice which has been given by expert grayling fishers for generations.

Finally, a question which perhaps should have been dealt with first: What determines whether or not a fly is a fancy pattern, or more to the point, a fancy grayling pattern? Take the Green Insect. It is a good caricature of the aphis and in that respect is as good an imitation as any trout pattern is of its relative natural. Given the chance, the trout will often confirm this too. Sturdy's Fancy was created as a trout pattern in the first place and, when it is well greased or oiled, it makes as good an imitation of a spinner as the Pheasant Tail Spinner, and who would call that valuable dressing a fancy pattern? The Treacle Parkin is prized highly as a trout fly for August and September both in Derbyshire and in Yorkshire, and the grayling are no more guilty than the trout in going for it if it is, indeed, nothing more than a fancy pattern.

In the case of a great many of the most popular and successful fly patterns, it is not known today what precisely the originators had in mind when they first tied them. He would be a brave man who would dare to arbitrate concerning the classification of artificials into fancy patterns and attempted imitations of naturals.

Similarly, to make any division of flies for grayling fishing, other than on the grounds of using a pattern because you have good reason to prefer it, has no genuine technical merit. Catching grayling on so-called fancy flies is great fun. Let us agree that – great fun – is what we are after, and let us say a word of thanks to those anglers of long ago who devised the patterns that have given so many grayling fishers so much pleasure over so many years.